T0341441

THE
SUPER
UPSIDE
FACTOR

Asymmetric Principles that Will **10X** Your Life

THE

SUPER

UPSIDE

FACTOR

DANIEL SHIN UN KANG

WILEY

Published by John Wiley & Sons, Inc., Hoboken, New Jersey.
Published simultaneously in Canada.

For general information on our other products and services or for technical support, please contact our Customer Care Department within the United States at (800) 762-2974, outside the United States at (317) 572-3993 or fax (317) 572-4002.

Wiley also publishes its books in a variety of electronic formats. Some content that appears in print may not be available in electronic formats. For more information about Wiley products, visit our website at www.wiley.com.

Library of Congress Cataloging-in-Publication Data

Names: Daniel Shin Un Kang, author.
Title: The super upside factor : applying asymmetric principles to 10x your life / Daniel Shin Un Kang.
Description: Hoboken, New Jersey : John Wiley & Sons, Inc., [2025] | Includes index.
Identifiers: LCCN 2024048506 (print) | LCCN 2024048507 (ebook) | ISBN 9781394254910 (hardback) | ISBN 9781394254934 (adobe pdf) | ISBN 9781394254927 (epub)
Subjects: LCSH: Success in business. | Success. | Risk.
Classification: LCC HF5386 .K1927 2025 (print) | LCC HF5386 (ebook) | DDC 650.1—dc23/eng/20241213
LC record available at https://lccn.loc.gov/2024048506
LC ebook record available at https://lccn.loc.gov/2024048507

Cover Design: Wiley
Author Photo: 시현하다 경미기록가

Printed and bound by CPI Group (UK) Ltd, Croydon, CR0 4YY

C9781394254910_03025

To my mom, dad,

and sister—you have been my greatest gift.

I love you, always.

Contents

PART

I | Asymmetric Principles

What if you're wrong?

It's a simple question, but the stakes couldn't be higher. In our most formative years, we're taught to strive for perfection. Praise follows each correct answer, while a big red F brands any mistake as a failure. The game we're taught assumes a known path, with success defined by a perfect score.

While the premise feels intuitive, it runs counter to how the most successful industries and careers rose to the top—by being wrong 90% of the time. Extraordinary outcomes are a game of outliers, driven by a handful of outsized events. We all know how a single accident can shatter your life, but the reverse is just as true. One pivotal encounter or timely decision can tilt your life to success. Picture your future balanced on a knife's edge, teetering between the ordinary and extraordinary, waiting for that one right move. What if your dreams were just a few moves away?

In Part I, we'll explore the counterintuitive strategies that power the world's biggest wins, even when most of their bets fail. By the end, you'll know how to apply these same principles to your own life, cutting through the noise to find the few moves that can tip your life toward something extraordinary. These are the *Asymmetric Principles*.

1 | The Few Right Things

Imagine a game, rigged in your favor. Every time you play, you can bet a single dollar with a binary outcome: win $1,000 or lose the dollar. Better yet, you can play the game as many times as you want. In this game, even if you're wrong 99% of the time, you'd still come out ahead. It feels almost too good to be legal.

This simple setup captures the essence of asymmetric payoffs, where the upside outsizes both the cost and the risk of the game. These asymmetric opportunities linger all around us, though often obscured by complexities. With a bit of precision, you'll see the hidden potential and hidden pitfalls disguised by averages. This game isn't just a clever thought experiment in a vacuum. This asymmetric principle is the foundation of trillion-dollar industries playing this rigged game every day: the world of venture capital and start-ups.

The Trillion Dollar Industry Paid to Be Wrong

Venture capital (VC) is probably one of the only industries in the world *paid to be wrong*. VC is a special type of financing that has more

3

than $2 trillion under management globally,[1] and deploys hundreds of billions annually.[2] It proliferated in the mid-1900s[3] to solve a circular problem of early-stage companies. Traditional forms of financing for companies often required proof of profitability and cash flow, but early-stage companies needed capital precisely *because* they didn't have predictable profitability and cash flow as they scaled. Hence the circularity.

Venture capitalists figured out that putting up capital for a special breed of companies—ones with potential to grow very big, very fast—can lead to phenomenally high returns. The few wins were so outrageously large that they would more than offset the losses, despite the high risk of early-stage companies without strong cash flows. To quantify just how big and how fast, I'm talking billions within a few years' time. Uber was started in 2009, hit a $3.5 billion valuation by 2013, and then crossed $50 billion in 2015.[4] Instagram was started in 2010, and acquired 18 months later for a billion dollars.[5] The recent AI boom has only accelerated the time to such valuations. In fact, if you observe the top 20 companies of the New York Stock Exchange, almost all of them have been funded by VCs. If the outcomes are so outsized when you're right, just how often can you be wrong and still make money in this industry? It turns out, quite a bit.

The 90% Failure Rate

An approximation circulated in the VC community around the success rates of their investments is the rule of thirds: make money on a third, break even on a third, and lose money on a third. But several empirical studies that examine the numbers from both academia and private research suggest that this adage may be wishful thinking.

The *Financial Times* shows the venture capital industry as a whole *loses money* more than 50% of the time.[6] Other analyses of venture funds, including the one by Correlation Ventures, recently shared that

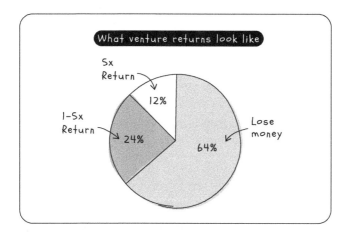

Figure 1.1   Venture Capital Returns, *Percentage as Number of Deals*

venture capital funds lose money on more than half of their deals, crunching 35,000 venture investments in the United States between 2013 and 2022[7] (see Figure 1.1).

For asymmetric outcomes to work, the upside needs to seriously outsize all other losses, so even a 5× return on investment is a generous definition of "hits." Even under such favorable definition, VCs fall short of their objectives 90% of the time, yet still make money. Asymmetric outcomes with outsized returns and minimal losses allow this dynamic to occur with a handful of wins.

Top-performing venture capital funds have just a few notable big wins that kicked off their legacy. Sequoia Capital is one of the oldest and most prestigious funds in the industry, managing about $85 billion.[8] Sequoia Capital was started in the 1970s by Don Valentine with $3 million.[9] Early investments in Apple and Atari put Sequoia on the map, before their other home runs in Google, Instagram, NVIDIA, and PayPal, among others. SoftBank Group, led by Masayoshi Son, hit a home run investing in Alibaba Group in 2000 for about $20 million, which grew into a $50 billion stake during Alibaba's IPO in

2014,[10] considered one of the most successful investments in the tech history. It's also the win that became a precursor to the largest technology focused venture capital fund in the world: SoftBank Investment Advisers, known as The Vision Fund, where I had the pleasure of working. These pivotal wins aren't just glories of the past. I'll walk through a more recent example, and work out the math.

The 1,000× Return

Overlooking the glowing terracotta rooftops, tinged orange by the sun dipping below the ocean, I sipped my espresso and savored a world-class Pastéis de Belém, its sweetness cutting through bitterness of the sip. Amidst the vibrant energy on the rooftops of Lisbon, I shared a co-living space with 10 strangers who quickly became friends. Little did I know that within a few months, one would benefit from one of the hottest tech stories of 2021: Figma.

Figma is a start-up that helps people collaborate on User Interface and User Experience design (UI/UX). At the risk of oversimplifying, UI is designing what your buttons look like, and UX is designing what happens when you click through the buttons. It's a part of every app, website, and really any digital interface you use today. Figma started more than a decade ago and raised their first venture capital round of $3.8 million in 2012, valued at $10.9 million led by Index Ventures.[11] All this means is that Figma traded a portion of their ownership or "equity" of the company in exchange for money today. In this case, Figma gave Index Ventures 35% ownership ($3.8 million over $10.9 million) in exchange for $3.8 million. Figma wasn't an obvious win.

For the first nine years, Figma didn't generate any cash, which might sound crazy. But then in 2021, the first year of making money, Figma generated $200 million in annual recurring revenue (ARR). In 2022, they doubled that number to $400 million,[12] continuing to grow to more than $600 million in 2023. It turned out to be a great investment for Index Ventures, because a decade after the investment,

Adobe offered to buy Figma for $20 billion, almost a 1,800× increase in value from the initial $10.9 million.

Twenty. Billion. Dollars. So, what happened to Index Ventures' $3.8 million? Well, simple math tells us that 36% of $20 billion is $7.2 billion. After adjusting for the annoying real-life details like dilution, it is estimated that the initial $3.8 million turned into about $2.6 billion[13] or 684× return on money. To illustrate it another way, if you had put in $1,500, you'd have a million dollars. While the deal ultimately fell apart due to antitrust regulations in Europe, you can see directionally how it would've been an extraordinary return. With Figma alone, Index Ventures could theoretically have been wrong 600 times on $3.8 million investments before being right, and they still would've made money. Even at the entire fund level, Index could have been wrong 100 times and still have dream returns for top VC funds.

These skewed upsides may seem like once-in-a-blue-moon type of events, but Figma isn't a standalone example. Venture capitalists and start-up founders have figured out how to repeatedly identify and generate these huge outcomes. LinkedIn[14] and GitHub[15] were acquired by Microsoft for $26 billion and $7.5 billion, respectively. Other start-ups became standalone, doing their IPOs like Uber (2019), Airbnb (2020), DoorDash (2020), Robinhood (2021), and Coupang (2021) that have all become multibillion dollar companies. VCs found a way to consistently identify and realize outsized returns, and my view is that we can too.

Asymmetric Outcomes for Life

The primary thesis of the book is that we can apply these proven principles used by investors to personal lives and careers. If the thesis is correct, then the extraordinary trajectory in your life will come down to the *few right things*, and less about getting everything right. The good news is that a considerable number of hyper-successful people attribute their success to these principles of asymmetry.

Jeff Bezos, in Amazon's 2014 Letter to Shareholders, shared the following: "Outsized returns often come from betting against conventional wisdom, and conventional wisdom is usually right. Given a 10% chance of a 100 times payoff, you should take that bet every time. But you're still going to be wrong nine times out of ten. . . . The difference between baseball and business, however, is that baseball has a truncated outcome distribution. When you swing, no matter how well you connect with the ball, the most runs you can get is four. In business, every once in a while, when you step up to the plate, you can score 1,000 runs."[16]

Bill Ackman, a billionaire and CEO of Pershing Square Capital Management, tweeted, "My best and favorite investments come from a deep understanding of the importance of asymmetry, that is, by understanding the potential risk and reward, and making sure that the reward overwhelming compensates for the risk. I have made some great asymmetric investments at Pershing Square, and also personally in start-ups. My first venture capital investment returned 1,650 times my initial investment."[17]

Nassim Nicholas Taleb, a trader and author of *The Black Swan*, shares this sentiment in his book: "The best description of my lifelong business in the market is 'skewed bets,' that is, I try to benefit from rare events, events that do not tend to repeat themselves frequently, but, accordingly, present a large payoff when they occur."[18]

Sam Altman, now the CEO of OpenAI, shared similar sentiments: "Optimize for being spectacularly right some of the time, and low stakes wrong a lot of the time."[19]

So at least anecdotally, applying mechanisms of asymmetry to individual lives and careers seems to work. It's a few of the right things that really elevated their success, rather than a gradual linear growth of hitting all the right boxes.

Why You Should Read On

Unfortunately, inspirational aphorisms, while motivational and true, rarely offer practical guidance. It's akin to the investment advice "buy low, and sell high," or in the start-up world, "find product market fit." These are technically correct statements, but, they're like a compass pointing to true north, without specifics on how to get there.

What I've aimed to do in these pages is create a playbook—the map to the compass so to speak. These principles are built not only on proven frameworks and research but also on real-time experiments in my own life across a diverse set of contexts, from a pilot sponsored by the Department of National Defence of Canada, venture capitalist at SoftBank Vision Fund, board advisor of a multibillion-dollar company, start-up co-founder backed by Y-Combinator, and an author published with Wiley. The collection of principles is what I call *Asymmetric Principles*.

What to Expect

The rest of the book is composed of three parts. The remainder of Part I will walk through the mechanics of *Asymmetric Principles*, first in context of venture capital, followed by specific adaptations and qualifiers needed to apply to individuals. Taking these basic building blocks, what follows are precise details, illustrated with real-time examples in my own life, from 15 minutes of writing investment that gave an outsized return of publishing with Wiley, all the way to career swings that enabled me to raise millions from top investors in the world. Details and qualifiers of these chapters is what will differentiate *Asymmetric Principles* from reckless risk taking.

Part II shifts gears to a step-by-step guide to start applying *Asymmetric Principles*. Taking *systems* as the unit of analysis, I discuss different types of systems required in stages of applying *Asymmetric Principles*, from the earliest stages of consistently identifying asymmetric opportunities; to maximizing luck of generating the initial traction; to scaling to the Super Upside with leverage; and finally to leaning in and out of different systems to work together with the rest of your life portfolio.

Finally, Part III discusses predictable problems that will arise as you start applying *Asymmetric Principles* in your life, including the exposure to higher stressors, and loss of agency that accompanies success. I follow that up with prescriptions to preemptively protect oneself, including a counterintuitive framework of quitting in the right way.

In the very next chapter, I'll dive into the basic building blocks of *Asymmetric Principles*. These fundamentals will serve as a foundation, expanding with precision in the chapters that follow.

2

Defining Asymmetric Principles

My heart skipped a beat. The sharp scent of burned rubber stung my nose, accompanied by the growl of the noticeably weary engine. My driver was overtaking a car at 200 km an hour, in the beaten-up, gray Volkswagen I had matched with at the airport. I clenched on to the handle as if it'd do any good. Despite the winter chill in Berlin I felt only a moment ago, I was sweating in the middle of the Autobahn—not just from the near collision of my Uber driver, but because of my destination: headquarters of Auto1. Auto1 is a multibillion-dollar company that facilitates online trade of used cars. It's also where I held my first formal board position—though as an observer—in my career.

A few weeks earlier, I had entered the rather dimly lit board room, and grabbed a Schnittchen—an open sandwich that was too dry for my tastes—before sitting down for the hours of discussion ahead. Surrounded by industry veterans advising boards of Lufthansa and Volkswagen, my only chance of adding any value to the discussion was to do considerable work ahead of time. After the routine financial updates for the quarter, we moved quickly to the critical agenda point on the next stage of the business. The two co-founders, Christian and Hakan, navigated the discussion with charisma and data you'd come to expect from veteran founders, addressing the pointed questions from the board with clarity. The conclusion was one we had predicted before the meeting began: more capital to fuel the next stage of growth—even after the hundreds of millions SoftBank had already invested into the business.

A few days after the meeting, the C-suite asked me to fly out to Berlin to work directly with the team on fundraising, so I packed my bags. As my Uber driver swung onto Bergmannstraße, I unclenched my hand from the handle. With relief, I stepped out of the car, headed to the now familiar café to order a flat white. I took the first sip for a brief moment of calm before addressing the elephant in my mind: Should we be doubling down?

Venture investment requires judgment. There should be a clear thesis on why and how a company will generate outsized returns for investors. At SoftBank, the stakes were hundreds of millions of dollars to fund. Yet decisions had to be made with incomplete information, and consequences were hard to reverse. What made it exceptionally challenging was the complexity in the number of variables to consider. What if cost of used cars goes up, which could cut into gross margins? What if the interest rates increase, which would require more liquidity? What if inventory cycles slow, which could require a larger financing facility? What if the company can't raise in time? Even with a few "What ifs," you can quickly see how there could be a near-infinite number of combinations of potential outcomes to consider. How does one cut through such complexity, never mind finding the perfect asymmetric opportunity for investments? And how does that translate to life decisions?

Identifying Asymmetric Opportunities

From the perspective of the present, every opportunity has a single realized past, and a range of possible future outcomes (Figure 2.1).

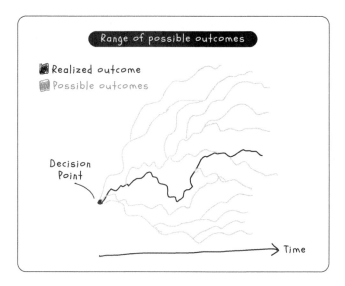

Figure 2.1 Range of Possible Outcomes

Each possible outcome has some probability of becoming the single realized path. And each realized path will impact you based on how you've positioned yourself. Let's call the range of possible outcomes variance; the associated probability frequency; and your position as impact. So if you're tossing a coin, variance is the range of possible outcomes, like heads, tails, and sides. Frequency is the probability, let's say it's roughly 49% chance of heads, 49% chance of tails, and 1% chance on side of the coin. And impact depends on how you've positioned yourself against the outcome, let's say a bet of $50 on heads.

Variance and frequency are objective measures, but impact is subjective based on your position. That is, the direction and magnitude of your impact is based on your position to the outcome. For example, if you toss a coin for fun, outcomes—heads, tails, or side—have no impact. In contrast, if you bet your net worth on heads for double or nothing, then outcomes will have a huge impact. Most investments are a more complex permutation of this base idea with a few more layers. Take, for example, stock market investing, and consider company performance relative to equity research analyst forecasts.

Your first-order impact, barring exceptions like a financial crisis, will, roughly speaking, resemble the following based on your position:

- You don't own any financial security: No real impact.
- You own the stock: If the company falls short or exceeds by the same amount, the impact would be relatively symmetrical.
- You bought a call option: Downside is usually limited to the premium, but the upside can be huge.
- You sold a call option: Upside is usually limited to the premium, but the downside can be huge.
- You short sold: Symmetrical impacts are amplified with leverage.

Investing in asymmetric opportunities works on the same basic principles, but has unique characteristics. First, the variance of outcomes is *far wider*. For asymmetric upsides, the upside outcomes disproportionately outsize the cost of investment and all possible outcomes, and vice versa for asymmetric downsides. The key is to find the upward asymmetry, so when you win, you win big, and when you lose, you don't lose much. Otherwise known as *skewed bets*, this is how investors benefit from asymmetric opportunities.

Cutting Through Complexity: Scenario Forecasts

The obvious problem is that multibillion-dollar decisions happen to be more complex than tossing a coin to assess if an opportunity is truly asymmetric. That's even more so with the considerable number of possible outcomes to consider from the endless "what ifs." One method investors used to cut through the complexity is sampled approximation, which we called *scenario forecasts*. Put simply, it's sampling the most material scenarios, out of the infinite possible outcomes. Typically, we sample at least three—though often much more—broad scenarios: upside case, base case, and downside case. These scenarios consider how multiple variables interact with each other to paint a real picture of what would happen, including a series of events that'd lead to said scenario. The approach gives a far more accurate and useful output for assessing an opportunity than thinking through an endless number of what ifs with single variables. I'll walk through a few concrete examples, particularly useful for the downside.

For emerging markets, rather than examining macroeconomic variables like interest rates, inflation, and defaults independently, we'd consider a scenario of "economic downturn." That's because it would be odd for heavy inflation to occur on its own without corresponding movement of interest rates, and default rates. Rather than running analyses of how a single variable would change the outcome and impact, we'd incorporate material variables including the devaluation of the foreign currency against the dollar (the investment currency), rising default rates, slowdown of sales, and interest rate movements.

We run scenario forecasts to paint an accurate picture to assess the downside, without underestimating or overestimating the downside. Variables interplaying during a downward spiral of an economic meltdown are far worse than what a single "what if" would estimate. At the same time, forecasting the series of events that'd take place avoids overestimating the downside from conflating mutually exclusive scenarios. For example, the devaluation of the local currency against the dollar would impact both the revenue base and cost base. I wouldn't assume sales to fall in terms of the US dollar while assuming the invoices from three months ago in local currency to somehow increase in terms of US dollars. In fact, if the company kept most of the investments in US dollars, as most are advised to do, that'd have greater buying power than before. The downside scenario isn't blindly stressing scenarios. It's replicating what such a scenario would represent, which cuts through the complexities to accurately evaluate the opportunity.

This is the sort of work I did as a venture capitalist, though in far more detail, when considering the investment decision. What happened to Auto1? We ended up doubling down and helped raise the 255 million euros, despite the capital scarcity that hit in 2020.

Worth the Work

The following year, I found myself enjoying a much more leisurely pace of life. Sitting in the meadows of Oxford, I relished the view of the river Cherwell, made even better with a sip of espresso after rowing practice at an ungodly early hour. A sense of satisfaction washed over me as I read the news on my phone: "Auto1 goes public," and at a valuation of almost $10 billion.[1] A single outsized return can be life changing, for both investors and for you.

While billion-dollar decisions sound grand, I'd argue that your personal life decisions hold far greater significance, in terms of subjective outcomes—you'd be the one living through it. Yet, when it comes to life decisions, the same level of rigor is often lacking. There is a tendency to be simplistic, from "lumping" outcomes into averages, reducing choices down to pros and cons lists, and using imprecise worst- and best-case scenarios. While that system of thinking suffices in most cases, where variance of outcomes is relatively narrow (as you'll see in Chapter 5), asymmetric opportunities definitionally require precision. Realizing these outsized returns requires a similar approach to how venture investors have consistently generated outsized returns. In the next section, I'll take this simple framework as a starting point before layering on details of applying such principles in personal life decisions over the rest of the book.

Asymmetry in Personal Lives

You and I are not venture funds. There are a host of differences from risk tolerance to, well, the fact these are real human beings, so certain adaptions are required for these principles to work for life decisions. By experimenting with these general principles in my own life, I arrived on adaptations and qualifiers needed for life decisions. Taking the scenario forecast as the first step, I've set precise definitional characteristics of asymmetric opportunities, which I've summarized as *Asymmetric Principles* in Table 2.1.

Table 2.1 **Summary of Asymmetric Principles**

Scenarios	Characteristics
• Upside	• Disproportionately outsizes both the investment and all other ranges of scenarios
	• Non-zero, visible path to realize the upside (Need-to-Believe)
	• Uncapped, without artificial barriers
• Base case	• Takes you where you want to go
• Downside	• Outcomes are tolerable
	• Outcomes are floored
	• Outcomes are predictable

Asymmetric Upside: Real, Uncapped, Opportunities

Asymmetric Upside or the Super Upside is a sampled outcome that has (1) a clear, non-zero probability path with (2) huge outcomes that outsize both your investment to take the shot and all other outcomes by several orders of magnitude. Let's start with the first qualifier.

When I share this definition, I see two flavors of pitfalls: On one hand, there is danger to see upsides as a license to defy laws of reality and common sense, calling impossible things upsides. That's daydreaming, not sampling an upside. On the other hand, there is fear from conflating the sheer size of the outcomes with the probability of the outcome that leads relegating the upside into the realm of impossibility, despite the fact there are possible paths to that upside that may materialize.

To avoid both errors, one framework I've borrowed from my time as an investor is called a *Need-to-Believe* analysis. Ask yourself the question "What are the set of assumptions I would need to believe for the upside to necessarily become true?" It's a common exercise for investors to write down a list of all assumptions that would need to be true for the upside to occur and then evaluate each assumption for its validity and probability. I'll take an example from the question I receive rather often: "Should I take this start-up job offer?"

Need-to-Believe Analysis   I had the same question in my second year as a management consultant. A recently funded start-up reached out to chat about a role as a Director of Strategy. At the time, I was at Oliver Wyman, which was a top strategy consulting firm globally. What would a *Need-to-Believe* analysis look like for this sort of life decision? For simplicity, I'll walk through this scenario assuming the financial upside as the material variable, which would be determined by at least two things: the future value of the company (pie) and projected ownership stake (your piece of the pie).

Let's start with the pie. Optimists may be thinking of people who became millionaires in recent years with companies like Uber or more recently NVIDIA. The minor detail here is that Uber's IPO valuation was $75 billion,[2] which at the time was the highest valuation in the IPO history of the New York Stock Exchange. And NVIDIA? Literally one of the most valuable companies in the world. The fact of the matter is that most companies will fail, and even those that succeed will probably not IPO at Uber's $75 billion valuation or grow to NVIDIA's $3 trillion valuation. For reference, David Friedberg, a founder of a billion-dollar company or "unicorn," shared that the chances are 0.00006%.[3] So you should have a good thesis as to why that company you're joining will be the exception to the rule. What are the minimum things that need to go right? Table 2.2 is a simplified example of the type of exercise you would go through to see what assumptions must be true for that start-up to become one of those unicorns.

Table 2.2 is overly simplified and ignores details like volatile valuation multiples, capital structures, cash flows, product cycle, and so on. You can go into tremendous amounts of details from historical valuation multiples to profit margin growth to sales efficiency to backgrounds of founders and so on. However, the example serves to roughly illustrate how you'd assess the size of the pie—to see if there is a real path toward an upside or not. We're not flying blind here.

Table 2.2 What Would It Take for the Company to Be Valued at $1 Billion?

Assumptions	Data	Assessment	Conclusion
• **Valuation:** Company will be valued at a 10 times multiple of its revenue	• Companies with similar model, industry, and profit margins trade 8–12 times the revenue	• Assumption is reasonable	• Company needs to generate $100 million in revenue
• **Price:** Company will continue to sell the product at current prices of $20	• Company sets the price on par with competitors at $20/ month to users in the country	• Assumption is validated	• Company needs to sell 417,000 units to generate $100 million of revenue
• **Units:** Company will sell 417,000 units	• There are 350,000 target users in the country	• Assumption is impossible even if they take 100% of the market	• Outcome is impossible with current prices and target customers

But let's suppose that the start-up where you work did beat the odds and became a unicorn. The other end of the equation is your share of the pie. Let's say your offer is for a mid-level business development position, and the package is 0.1% share of the company. That means if the company becomes valued at $1 billion, you'd take home about $1 million (I recognize this is the best case if we ignore details such as dilution, vesting periods, and seniority at liquidation that would reduce your share of the pie). That, by the way, gives no prescription on how long it'll take to get there. Even with this simple back-of-the-envelope work, assessing an opportunity becomes easier. Now you can start to ask the question if that is a number you'd consider as an outsized return given your cost of investment (leaving your current job or taking a different offer) and all predictable ranges of outcomes. For some it is, and for others, it isn't.

So, did I take the offer? To be clear, the message was not an offer, but an interview, which I ended up declining. A few years later, I'd read about that start-up going public. When I did some quick math after the fact, I probably missed out on a few million dollars. While hindsight is 20/20, running a *Need-to-Believe* analysis would've provided me a much more accurate assessment of the upside, and the core assumptions to at least take that interview, especially if I saw a clear, non-zero path to the upside. The second qualifier for asymmetric upsides is a large, uncapped one.

Large, Uncapped Upside as a Function of Rapid Growth
Recently, a Korean pop singer created history on Billboard. Jungkook, from BTS, became the fastest to hit a billion streams on Spotify—in 108 days[4]—with his single "Seven." In a little more than three months, he had a billion people listening. But maybe that's not relatable to you and me. Afterall, most of us don't have a record label, fan base, and an army of people to make that happen.

But what about Billie Eilish? In 2016, as a 14-year-old, she uploaded her debut single *Ocean Eyes* to SoundCloud that went viral overnight.[5] As of August 2024, the song has more than 500 million streams on the official YouTube music video and 1.5 billion streams on Spotify.[6] Today, she's considered one of the most successful pop artists of our time. To be clear, this is not to undermine hard work and talent in the name of luck. Rather, it's to illustrate what a large, uncapped upside looks like in asymmetric upsides.

Imagine if there was a group of people huddled around a board room saying, "Hmm, she's a bit too young to be getting billions of streams, why don't we replace her with another artist who's spent a few more years grinding?" or "He needs a PhD or some formal education before hitting a billion streams. You know, some foundational stuff." Or "There's been too many pop streams lately. Why don't we take this song off and replace it with some jazz?" That would be ridiculous. Don't tolerate ridiculousness in your life. Upsides shouldn't have artificial barriers.

A natural consequence of large, uncapped upsides is the implied speed of their growth rate. You cannot hit a billion streams from 1,000 streams a day—that'd take you more than 2,700 years. While I'll discuss naturally scalable forms of growth in Chapter 7, asymmetric upsides necessarily embed an explosive growth rate.

To eventually reach the Super Upside, *Asymmetric Principles* requires the upside to have a clear, non-zero probability path to a large, uncapped upside. Even if you don't realize your upside, *Asymmetric Principles* requires that your most likely outcomes propel you forward, not backward.

Asymmetric Base Case: Leading Where You Want to Go

Asymmetric base case is a sample of the most likely outcome from your scenarios. The most important qualifier is that this needs to *take you where you want to go.* The upside would take you there a lot faster, but the base case should directionally place you on the same path, even if it takes you a few more steps. In other words, swinging for the fences at the expense of your base case falls outside the scope of *Asymmetric Principles.* One of the most pertinent characteristics of the base case is surviving for a long time even if your upside doesn't happen for a long time, as many founders come to understand.

In start-up land, Y-Combinator (YC) is the most sought-after accelerator in the world, having incubated category-defining companies like Airbnb, DoorDash, Stripe, and Coinbase. Just this year, YC expanded their program from two to four cohorts a year, which means companies can apply roughly four times a year to be a part of the program.

Suppose that two founding teams consider YC as their upside case and building a functional company that covers its cost (without salary) as their base case. The first founding team all quit their full-time jobs with six months of savings and work full-time on building their company. The second founding team continues to advance their careers and build larger savings while spending their weekends on building their company. For the first six months, the former probably has a higher probability of joining YC and realizing their base case faster. But what about over a time horizon of a year or two or five? On a time scale of five years, the second group would have 10 times the number of shots at applying to YC than the first. Assuming they continued to talk to customers and build their product, the second group would, generally speaking, push their base case forward to build a company even without YC. All the while, they would continue to retain the option to go all in, under more favorable conditions with more savings, a larger network, and better product.

That is not to say you shouldn't ever take risks or big swings. In fact, in the very next chapter, I share how to take larger risks under *Asymmetric Principles*. But ruining your base case in the name of going after the upside is a crude way to approach risk and falls outside the definition of *Asymmetric Principles*. It can work for a small number of people, but so does the lottery. The base case is not a throwaway case. It should serve as a solid path to get you where you want to go, even if your upside isn't realized for a particular shot. This idea of surviving relates directly to the downsides as well.

Asymmetric Downside: Floored, Tolerable, and Predictable

"You play it too safe" was a common criticism I received growing up. Ironically, it's this risk aversion that enabled me to ultimately start my own company, raise capital from YC, and survive tech valuation crash and digital bank runs over the last few years. Asymmetric downsides run exactly against the spirit of "high risk, high reward," which simply looks at the proportion of the upside to the potential downside. Asymmetric downsides are distinct in that they need to be floored, tolerable, and predictable regardless of how great the potential upside can be, because you need to be alive.

Floored, Tolerable Downside   The most important qualifier for the downside is that it is *tolerable* for you. Remember that while outcomes and probabilities are objective, the impact on you is subjective. The exact set of outcomes that is tolerable for some may be intolerable for others. Non-tolerable downsides fall outside the definition of *Asymmetric Principles* for at least two reasons.

First, if you're trading potential catastrophic downsides for spectacular upsides, that's a symmetric trade-off. You're risking just as much as you're potentially gaining. Second, *Asymmetric Principles* is *iterative* in nature. As you saw from the earlier examples with venture capital, a single loss should not ruin the fund. *Few Right Things* from Chapter 1 implies that you have the capacity to take the other 99 times that don't work out for that one Super Upside. For many people, failing once in a major life decision can be so detrimental to their lives that they can never take another swing again. Those types of downsides fall outside the scope of *Asymmetric Principles*, which is why it's designed to allow even the smallest of investments to grow big.

Recognize also that these downsides aren't static and can change over time depending on the evolution of your situation, macro environment, and refined information. That means downsides can become intolerable over time. Opportunity cost is a great example of this. Spending a year on a project can be a floored, tolerable downside. Spending two decades may not. Many people accidently do this. Ensure that the downside is floored to the tolerable level. What you don't want as a downside is a bottomless pit that can not only destroy your life but also the lives of your loved ones.

Reasonably Predictable   To ensure the downside is tolerable and floored, it follows you'd have to know what the downsides are. Minimize the unknown unknowns when it comes to the downsides, and forecast scenarios within bounds of *reasonable probability*. By reasonable probability, I mean not wasting brain space on apocalyptic events. Barring decisions that somehow directly raises chances of fatality or catastrophes, the rationale for excluding these in your downside is this: if the world is ending, you'll have bigger fish to fry anyway.

Similar to the *Need-to-Believe* analysis of the upside, the downside should be forecasted with precision and validated assumptions of how it will play out. What is the sequence of events that will lead to the downside? Accurately understanding the downside allows greater maneuverability. The intuition is like telling jokes without crossing the line of being offensive. You can take more risks with people you know intimately than a stranger on the streets. The better you understand the parameters of your downside, the greater risk you can take.

Perhaps more importantly, when you understand your downsides, you can place measures to avoid the downside, ahead of time. In other words, you can frontload exactly what needs to be done when you have time and mental capacity, rather than relying on your judgment during times of turmoil with emotionally charged chaos. The important piece is isolating the problem-solving from execution.

A common example is what behavior economists and game theorists call *precommitments*.[7] These are tested strategies, where you bind your future self today, based on downsides you predict in the future. Jon Elster notably talks about the famous Ulysses pact based on Homer's *The Odyssey*. On his journey back to his hometown after the victory of the Trojan War, Odysseus (or Ulysses) is warned of sirens' irresistible singing that lured sailors to steer their ships toward wreckage. Odysseus orders his crew to plug their ears with beeswax. But because he wanted to hear the beautiful singing, he orders the crew to tie him tightly to the mast while his crew steers the ship to safety.[8] These precommitments aren't restricted to theories or epics but used in practice. Traders, for example, place stop-loss orders to cap their losses ahead of time (automatically selling a stock when it falls below a predetermined value), helping them guard against cognitive biases—strongly at play as their position is falling—like loss-aversion and sunk cost fallacies.

Asymmetric Principles requires that you survive. By precisely predicting the downside, and choosing floored, tolerable ones, you can protect yourself from catastrophic outcomes and place mechanisms to escape the downside.

Just Getting Started

This chapter provided the most basic building blocks of *Asymmetric Principles* that'll serve as a foundation for the rest of the book. As mundane as they may sound, upside case with a clear, non-zero probability path to a large, uncapped rapid growth; base case that brings you where you want to go; and downside case that are floored, tolerable, and predictable are details and qualifiers are essential to *Asymmetric Principles* that work for life decisions. For readers familiar with these concepts, I hope you appreciate how the details come in to play over the course of the book. For readers who are less familiar, you may be wondering if there is such a thing as asymmetric opportunities in your life. The game can seem too rigged in your favor to be true. If it did exist, why haven't you seen it?

Well, it turns out most standalone choices in life aren't perfectly asymmetric opportunities, served up on a silver platter. Like investors, there is a considerable amount of work and optimization to get to the few right things. In the next chapter, I will detail my own real-time experiments I'm running with *Asymmetric Principles* in action in varying levels of risks and investments so that almost anyone can get started: from a small 15-minute investment of my time that led to a book deal with Wiley to betting my entire career to raise millions for my company.

3 | Dogfooding in Public

Eating your own dog food refers to using your own products and services before sharing them with others. It's commonly done in start-ups to fix any bugs and build confidence before releasing to the public. Anyone can have an abstract theoretical discussion on what should work, and it can be convincing when told in the right way. Dogfooding puts rubber to the road and sees how things hold in reality with skin in the game. That's what I've done with *Asymmetric Principles* in my own career and life.

Why did it apply in some contexts and not others? What were the limitations? What did the framework miss? The specific qualifiers from Chapter 2 didn't come from some imaginary thought experiment, but from data-backed research along with my own experiments. To do one better, I've included this chapter to *build in public* in real time.

Building in public has become common in the start-up world, where founders publicly share their journey—both errors and corroborations of their hypotheses. Building in public allows founders to share findings with the community to increase the cumulative pace of learning, which

I encourage you to do by sharing your stories at www.thesuperupside .com. Perhaps more importantly, it requires founders to put their reputation on the line, as I'm doing with mine. After a decade of experimentation, I have enough conviction in *Asymmetric Principles* to build in public despite my natural reticence.

This chapter is publicly dogfooding *Asymmetric Principles*, where I'll share two real-time examples in my own life—both of which will be under way by the time the book is released. The first example illustrates how the tiniest investment can yield Super Upsides. My goal here is to proactively tackle proportionality bias, the misconception that large outcomes require equally large investments, and to encourage even the most risk-averse and even risk-restricted individuals to start making asymmetric bets. The second example takes the opposite approach: a career bet driven by conviction. It'll demonstrate how I used *Asymmetric Principles* to do conventionally "risky" things and realized the Super Upside without risking everything. Let's start with small.

15 Minutes to Be a Wiley Author

Most people can find 15 minutes a day to work on their dreams. For many aspiring authors, writing a book with a major publisher is a dream that can take years of hard work—writing the manuscript, editing it countless times, pitching to agents and editors, and finally landing that book deal. But by applying *Asymmetric Principles*, I bypassed this entire process. No manuscript. No agent. No pitch. In fact, it was the publisher who reached out to me to write a book, not the other way around. That's extraordinary luck, and here's how I maximized luck with a few minutes a day.

Writing for me started as an outlet to organize turbulent thoughts and emotions from the journey of starting a company. In my own community of founders, sharing these organized thoughts was well received. Over time, I saw patterns of problems and discussions, at which point I started to share my writing that gained some traction in the tech community. In the spring of 2022, I ran my own scenario forecast and decided to invest the little time I could afford into writing. I started with one six-hour Saturday session a month, writing on an online platform called Medium, which cost about one flat white at a typical London café. Daily, that came out to about 15 minutes and 16 cents. Here's the most candid recollection of the scenario forecasts I had at the time.

Base Case: Publisher–Backed Author

My base case was to write a book at some point, with a vague timeline of 5 to 10 years. While the timeline was vague, I did have a reasonable plan to craft a base case that would lead me where I wanted to go. Specifically, it was building up two important pieces for the success of any book: good content and good distribution.

Validating Demand for Content   Tucked within the chaos of downtown Los Angeles is an overhyped shop called *The Last Book Store*. My best friend from college was showing me around. He'd grown rounder since graduating and was breathing heavily as we climbed the stairs. I pointed it out, and he shot back, "how dare you." After passing the Instagramable decor, I noticed a wall of books hidden in a corner with a sign that said, "All books 25¢." Blank pages would be worth more than that. Some were hard covers too. I couldn't help but think "How bad does the book have to be for it to have *negative value?*"

My base case was writing content that is actually valuable to people. To validate that, I broke down a few topics into "mini chapters," which could potentially be part of a book. Each article was effectively an experiment to gauge which content resonated most with readers, and who my readers even were. The plan was to compile the best of these chapters for a book for the audience I had identified. Writing 2,000-word essays, rather than committing to a 60,000-word book right away, gave me maneuverability. To be precise, at least 29 more cycles with the same word count to publish, learn, and refine my writing. Comments, highlights, likes, and shares would be signals to validate that content was valuable for readers. Keeping a writing cadence of once a month with no real deadlines also gave me plenty of time to take note of the types of questions and discussions I observed from people around me. So by the time I started writing, I usually knew at least a few people who specifically wanted to hear what I had to say on a particular topic. Under this setup, I'd most probably hit the first part of my base case of writing valuable content. But even if I write valuable content, it wouldn't mean very much if no one read it. That's where the second part of my base case kicks in: distribution.

Building an Audience   Owning your audience was a hot topic with a major surge of the Creator Economy in 2020, a year before I officially entered the space. The idea was to distinguish *exposure* provided by platforms from *direct access* to your audience. For example, creators couldn't reach out to fans independently—like emails and texts—without the use of major social platforms. Building your own audience spoke to independence of creators from platforms, which directly applies to my own base case.

Having my own audience would mean I can always share valuable content with my readers without technical restrictions or censorships of gatekeepers. My work would be judged solely by my audience. To craft my base case—make it the most probable outcome—I'd need to get to a sizeable number of online. Locking in this base case would also raise the quality of my outcomes, including the chance to work with top book publishers.

In every negotiation table, I've found a position of leverage comes when you don't need the other party. When a start-up can profitably build without VCs, VCs come knocking with termsheets. When a musician goes viral without record labels, labels approach with a record deal. When authors can sell books without publishers, publishers pursue a book deal. Hitting my base case of building an audience would elevate my future base cases, maximizing "luck" of not only convincing a major publisher to publish my book, but also put their promotion behind it.

Publishers have a lot of levers to push your book, from organizing book tours, securing media coverage, and promoting through partners. If they don't put their money behind it, it's often a matter of incentives, not capacity. Everyone moves on incentives. The art of persuasion mostly comes down to finding and aligning incentives of parties. And any distributor, including major publishers, wants to make money. That means demonstrating the ability to sell. As they say, it's the best-selling author not the best-writing author. For publishers, it has to make economic sense for them to push. Putting myself in their shoes, there are probably at least two thresholds to cross.

1. **Returns:** Marketing investment in my book will lead to a positive return.
2. **Opportunity cost:** Marketing investment in my book will generate *best* positive returns among other books releasing on similar dates.

Having my own audience provides evidence to publishers that it'd be worth their time and investment. In addition, having data like views, comments, and engagements on "mini chapters" would provide stratified feedback on my writing for a compelling case on which topics might do well.

All along my base case, it didn't hurt that Medium offers a partnership program that pays out to writers like me. So far, it's earned enough to cover my coffees for the next few years. So not a bad base case. And then there is the downside.

Downside: Predictable, Tolerable Floors

At first glance, the downside of writing online didn't seem so high. The commitment I made was $5 and 6 hours a month. That comes to about $60 and 72 hours a year. That's fine.

Hold on. 72 hours.

That's a lot of time. That's a full work week in my life. I could do a lot if I had a full week of uninterrupted time. The opportunity cost to invest that much time was high, considering the fact I'm working on my start-up. I'd need to ensure that the downside is tolerable.

The most evident downside scenario was investing a significant amount of time and having none of my base cases play out. It'd be an awful waste of time if I couldn't validate the value of my writing or build my distribution. While 72 hours is more than I'd want to invest, a few things made the downside tolerable for me. The first was the reversible nature of this commitment. If I had no feedback from readers or building a following in, say, six months, I could always pull the plug, which would reduce my cost to about half the time, or 36 hours. That's three full workdays for me. The second was the nature of assets—which I'll share in detail in Chapter 7—I'd be creating through publishing my writing online. Published catalog content or *media assets* are nonrivalrous (several people can view it at the same time), nonexhaustible (does not wear out when it's used), and fungible (can be adapted into different forms). Put simply, if I publish my writing online, I'd be building a catalog of assets that are conducive to creating value continually in the future. So even in the downside scenario, my writing can be discovered and popularized in the future; repurposed into other forms like posts, tweets, podcasts, and videos; and published as a book should I choose to do so.

But what about more severe downside scenarios like getting sued for accidental copyright infringement? Or ruining my reputation from bad writing? I didn't see these as real downside scenarios. Recall that predictable downside scenarios shouldn't conflate mutually exclusive scenarios. I can't have zero readers of my content and simultaneously have my content ruin my reputation at scale. And if I did grow so spectacularly that experts noticed me, then I'd probably have robust systems in place to prevent that from happening. So, the downside was predictable, floored, and tolerable.

Upside: Accelerating the Path to Authorship

My sampled upside scenario—I had in my mind was condensing the 5- to 10-year time frame of my base case to a much shorter timeline, and publishing with one of the majors. My *Need-to-Believe* for this particular scenario would require at least the following series of events:

1. I write content that is sufficiently valuable, and commercial
2. I can reliably distribute my writing to a large number of people
3. I find the right "fans" who love my writing
4. I iterate the process with improvements and build a large audience in a short amount of time

If I could consistently hit all four, then I'd reach my upside. What played out was not this particular upside. Instead, writing online led to a few speaking engagements. In one event, an acquisition editor from Wiley—who happened to have worked in start-ups, and was familiar with start-up dynamics—was in the audience. She liked what I had to say and reached out for a book deal. From a timeline perspective, I started writing intentionally in March 2022, and I had a book deal in hand by August 2023, so the process took about 18 months. All in all, I directionally realized my upside, just in a different way. A single Saturday a month, equivalent of 15 minutes a day, is all it took.

In Chapter 1, I stressed the importance of a few right things. The one upside dramatically elevated my future set of possible outcomes from when I started. My new downside is becoming a published author with one of the majors; and my new upside is quite literally a Super Upside, ranging from building a media company to landing mainstream shows. We'll see how this real-time experiment plays out. My intent is not to be obnoxious about a win, but to drive the point you truly need just a few of these upsides for your own Super Upside, whether it's a small bet or a big one as you'll see in the next section.

Broadening the Definition of Starting

One final thought I'll end on this example is this: Be generous with the definition of starting. Starting can be as modest, inconsistent, and incomplete as you want it to be. If you check out my Medium account, I wrote my first piece in the fall of 2021. I was living in a house with a community of founders and content creators at the time. One creator, who became one of my best friends, nudged me to write just one article. His perspective, that I'm the utmost expert in my own experience, helped me overcome my fear of looking like a fool, which was a barrier to publishing my thoughts publicly. But it's not as if I wrote consistently after that one moment. I stopped, writing on and off for months without a set timeline or plan. That's a part of the starting journey. Sometimes starting just means planting a seed. That's the benefit of *Asymmetric Principles*. It's designed to start as small or as big as you want. A few years before my book, in 2020, I decided to go big, making a bet on *Asymmetric Principles* with my entire career.

Taking a Full Swing

People called me an idiot. Clutching the small, soulless cardboard box, I stepped down the two uneven stairs onto 69 Grosvenor Street. I paused to unbutton my overly tight shirt and fixed my coat, before walking down to *The Connaught Bar*—a place I'd often host friends, surrounded by the gleam of luxury in the heart of Mayfair. But that day, I turned the corner away from opulence into an unassuming green space that had become a refuge during my time alone in London. The air felt alive and brisk, the sunlight bronzing the leaves, marking the change of seasons—for me, and for the city. Yet even the serenity of the park couldn't silence the blaring, obnoxious question that screamed in my mind: "Am I really an idiot?"

In 2020, I left my job as a venture capitalist at SoftBank Investment Advisers. It was the golden years of venture capital, and SoftBank Investment Advisers or *The Vision Fund* came in swinging as the largest VC fund in the world, managing more than $100 billion.[1] My career trajectory at the fund was promising, too. Within the first few weeks of starting my role in the Bay Area, I was offered a job internally to join a team at the London headquarters because of an analysis I had done on a deal. A few months later, I became one of the only associates at the firm to hold a formal board, though observer, position. There was a clear path to progression within the organization. On top of that, as many familiar with the industry know, the salary and lifestyle were probably some of the best anyone could ask for in a job.

Understandably, departing SoftBank came with considerable concern from my peers, friends, mentors, and family about throwing away this opportunity to launch a start-up that provided nothing close in salary, prestige, lifestyle, progression, or really anything. It also didn't help that start-ups fail more than 90% of the time.[2] For similar reasons, I had also initially written off entrepreneurship as too risky. I could never relate to the biographies of famous entrepreneurs who risked their houses, health, families, and the shirts off their back to go all in on a company, like the one from *Shoe Dog*, the story of Phil Knight's journey of creating Nike. In my defense, and in defense of many like me, there is a difference between risk appetite and *risk restriction*. Not everyone can take such aggressive risks. It is not to downplay the risk, grit, and ambitions of other entrepreneurs, but many people simply cannot afford the *"Try, try again until you succeed"* model. As a risk-averse person, I thought deeply before taking this swing, because I knew I had to take a different approach than these entrepreneurs.

Recognizing Risk Restrictions

Not everyone comes from a background that is conducive to starting a company. There might be issues related to relationships, finances, health, or any number of reasons that add up to too much risk. While *Asymmetric Principles* can start as small as 15 minutes of time a day, making career bets requires time to build a foundation to be able to take risks.

In my case, the restriction was financial. I became the breadwinner for my family early on in my life. If I started and failed a company, I wouldn't mind sleeping on friends' couches. But maxing out my credit cards, missing rent payments, and having my parents and sister out on the streets was not a risk I was able to take. There was no safety net. I was the backstop. I had to take time to de-risk. My friends from my first consulting job know that I've wanted to start my own company. That was 2016. But it wasn't until 2021 that I pulled the trigger. For five years, I was intentional about choosing careers that optimized for three things:

1. Build a financial safety net for my family quickly (high-salaried jobs).
2. Build sector expertise for an area of my interest (fintech and marketplaces).
3. Build a network of friends and colleagues for a running start when I finally did begin my start-up.

In Chapter 2, I mentioned that perfectly asymmetric opportunities with great returns with minimum downsides aren't just sitting around. They often require optimizations. Optimizations are small adjustments to make an opportunity fall within definitions of *Asymmetric Principles*. Applying *Asymmetric Principles* with optimizations allowed me to take this conventionally risky career swing and make a bet on myself, even with my level of risk aversion with limited resources.

Fast-forward three years, was I an idiot to leave my job and start my company? As I rewrite this chapter overlooking Blue Bay in Mauritius, I'm wrapping up my day's work for my start-up with more than $3 million backed by top investors, including Y-Combinator. Here's how I optimized my scenarios to start my company from my grad school dorm room.

Optimize Downsides: No-Loss Scenarios

My favorite position in chess is called a fork. It's a tactical move where a single piece simultaneously attacks two or more of the opponent's pieces. As a novice player, I can't force my opponent into *which* piece to give up, but I know I'll take *a piece* from this move. Roughly speaking, I can't determine which *exact outcome* will occur, but I can determine which *set of outcomes* will. That's sort of how you want to forecast your downsides. You may be unsure which downside will play out, but you can anticipate which set of downside scenarios will occur, and each should leave you in a tolerable position.

Initially, the downside of starting a company was predictable, but not tolerable. Spending several years on a failed start-up, going into debt, and leaving my family unsupported was not an option I was willing to entertain. I also had to consider the high opportunity costs like continuing my career as an investor, joining a promising portfolio company, or moving to another role to learn something new. For the downside to fit the definition of *Asymmetric Principles*, I optimized the downside, by raising the floor. For people who are risk-restricted like me, it takes intention and time to progressively raise the downside floor, until you reach *a no-loss scenario.*

Tranching Investments Tranching is the first lever I used to optimize my downside. It's a way I've structured deals as an investor to minimize risk. Put simply, it's investing a small amount of capital to see time-based milestones, with the *right* to invest more in the future. If certain milestones aren't hit, then I wouldn't exercise that right to invest.

A classic example of this applied to personal careers is working on a side hustle, growing it to a certain threshold, and then investing more time, before leaving a full-time job. Unfortunately, a side hustle was not an option when working the intense hours in growth equity investment was already devouring me.

Instead, my tranche was time-based. I bought myself about 18 months' worth of savings that would fund my family. With that timeline in mind, my first tranche was a 10-month period with the milestone of raising money for my company. That way, I could pay myself to sustainably work on my startup. Fixing the milestone at 10 months floored my downside to sustain my family, with an 8-month buffer to find an income source even if it didn't work out. It also kept my opportunity cost in check with a minimal amount of time invested.

However, tranching to raise the floor comes with clear trade-offs. It *compresses variance* of both the upside and downside outcomes. For example, extending the timeline from 10 months to, say, 20 or 30 months would increase my probability to find the idea, develop a team, and secure the investment. Setting a tranche at 10 months simply may not be enough time for luck to find its way to me. But that was the best I could do for a tolerable downside given my restrictions. But this alone wouldn't create a no-loss scenario. With my floor raised to a tolerable level, I built in a contingency to further optimize my big career swing.

Buying Exit Options   In the 1970 Apollo 13 mission, an oxygen tank in the service module exploded, crippling the spacecraft and causing loss of oxygen and power. With their air supply dwindling, the astronauts repurposed the lunar module, originally designed for moon landings, to serve as a lifeboat (though it wasn't the intention), allowing them to return safely to Earth.[3] Now, I'm not so out of touch with reality to suggest my career decision is anything like the heroic feats of the Apollo 13 astronauts. But, the significance of contingencies stands, which often require preparation far in advance, which was 2018 for me.

When I received my offer to join SoftBank in 2018, I had a few competing offers. From my perspective, SoftBank was riskier than joining an established tech company. The Vision Fund had only closed their first round of funding in May 2017,[4] with little track record. When I accepted the offer, I built in a contingency. A few months into the job, I bought an exit option by applying to a Public Policy program at the University of Oxford. Not only was this a topic of interest, but the specific program had a practical requirement with a strong internship-matching program for candidates in the summer before graduating—it'd be unlikely I'd be left without a job. These types of contingencies need to be placed ahead of time. The temptation is to ignore its need over time. I urge you not to do this. Contingencies are underappreciated, precisely because they are rarely needed. They seem wasteful until the one time they are absolutely needed.

To be clear, I didn't leave SoftBank to escape, but I did repurpose my contingency exit option to elevate my downside floor when starting my company. Effectively, I raised the floor of my downside to getting an Oxford degree if my start-up failed in 10 months. The cherry on top was the resources and funds available to student entrepreneurs, which further helped me get going.

Asymmetric Principles can enable even the most risk-averse people like me to take large swings. While optimizations will take time, you'll eventually create a downside that is floored, tolerable, and predictable to make big bets.

The No-Loss Scenario Tranches and contingencies are just two examples of how taking a little time and intention can elevate the downside of large bets into predictable, tolerable floors. By tranching my investment, and repurposing contingency, my downside became a set of no-loss scenarios. I raised the floor from a bottomless pit of debt and wasted years, to a time-boxed 10-month period where my worst-case scenario was an Oxford graduate degree and a job while taking a stab at starting a company. That's a pretty damn good downside. But taking my career swing wasn't solely to avoid personal bankruptcy, but to build a successful company. Once my downside had a solid floor, I thought about optimizing my upside of raising that pre-seed: by maximizing luck.

Optimizing Upsides: Maximize Surface Area of Luck

With a whopping $200 million deal, Justin Bieber, the Canadian icon of pop music, broke a record in 2023. He sold his publishing and royalty rights to Hipgnosis Song Fund, now owned by the private equity fund Blackstone.[5] For anyone familiar with the pop world, you'll know Bieber's discovery story by Scooter Braun. Scooter Braun is one of the most prominent talent managers in the industry, managing artists like Arianna Grande, Demi Lovato, and Martin Garrix.[6] The publicized narrative is that Scooter accidentally clicked on Justin's YouTube video in 2008,[7] thinking it was someone else. That one "accident" led to one of the largest pop stars in the world closing out the $200 million deal. These fortunate coincidences are not unique to Justin Bieber, from Billie Eilish's viral Soundcloud post to Harrison Ford's carpentry work that led to *Star Wars*,[8] countless stories of serendipity are told. Whether you take these stories at face value or not, it's true that almost everyone ascribes some part of their success to luck. You can perceive it as modesty, or more cynically, a scripted answer prepared by a PR agency.

My view is that "luck" is shorthand for what actually happened. In every one of these stories, many omit a minor detail: the optimizations for finding that luck. Harrison Ford, for example, shared in an interview that he took the carpentry job to consistently take shots at being an actor through auditions while supporting himself and his family. Many founders raised their companies out of near-death situations with lucky encounters with investors, simply by moving to San Francisco. In the start-up world, we call this *maximizing the surface area of luck*. It is a common concept to position oneself in the way of luck.

In the context of my career decision, my upside was raising venture funding within the 10-month time. If I could pull it off, I'd be paid to work on solving a problem that I believed would change the world. How did I get in the way of luck? Of the many strategies, I'll share two that maximized my luck that led to more than $5 million in written commitments in a single week: Linearly stacking and changing systems.

Linearly Stacking Your Odds to the Limit Early-stage venture capital funds describe their work as finding a needle in the haystack. Sampling of a few publicly available statistics, pre-seed investment as a percentage of pitch meetings comes to roughly 0.2%, or roughly one in every 500 companies they meet.

My first optimization for my pre-seed was to linearly stack the odds in my favor. Some people may call this a "numbers game." I don't like that term because it's not precise. Remember that the upside needs to have a non-zero path to realize. That means meeting a minimum requirement for an investment, with a non-zero chance of a meeting leading to an actual investment. Pitching a company that is not designed to grow quickly—the requirement for the VC model to work—is a waste of time. Setting up a meeting with investors who don't invest in the stage or industry is a waste of time. It's not about simply going through the motions without thoughtfulness. When I set up these meetings, I hit minimum thresholds. Then came the probabilities.

Crudely assuming I'm an average pre-seed company, every "N" meeting would give me about roughly a 0.2% chance of investment. An intuitive way to increase luck that works is a simple stacking of odds by increasing the N. Or stacking as many of these shots for non-zero upsides as possible. To be clear, stacking N doesn't

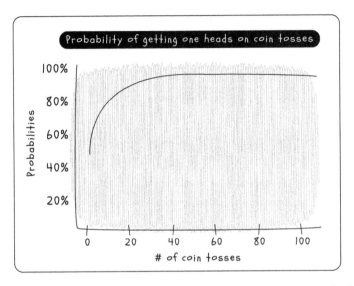

Figure 3.1   Probability of Getting at Least One Heads in 100 Fair Coin Tosses

guarantee anything. Elementary statistics tells us flipping a fair coin twice does *not* mean you'll have certainty of getting heads. That's not how probabilities work. But we do know that a game with 100 coin flips will have a higher chance of getting *at least* one heads than a game with a single flip. In fact, when I simulate the "probabilities of getting at least one heads" in 100 fair coin tosses, it graphs an asymptotic function with a limit of one or 100% (see Figure 3.1). Probability of getting at least one heads is the complement of getting tails every time, which is $1 - 0.5^{100}$. So statistically, it's almost "certain" I'll end up with at least one heads.

And that's exactly what I did. During my pre-seed round, I emailed several hundred investors, secured more than 160 meetings (coin tosses), and received an offer on meeting number 158. Effectively, I manufactured the "coin toss" mechanics for my fundraise, which directionally follows the probabilities of the coin toss model though in different magnitude. With every meeting or toss, I linearly increased my luck of an investment.

Limits of Linear Stacking However, stacking the odds will, at best, linearly increase your luck to a small degree, and realistically never reach the limits of "certainty" seen in the coin toss for at least two reasons. First, the strength of introductions will deteriorate with the increase of N. If your first meeting is your rich family member and your 100th meeting is your friend's sister-in-law's former boss's daughter who works as an analyst at a VC fund, what's the quality of that intro? The probabilities generally deteriorate with every N. The second reason, and perhaps a more glaring limitation, is that the probabilities are too low for the Ns to be stacked. If the probability of getting my first investment is 0.2%, every incremental N meeting would increase my chances. It would take well more than 1,000 quality Ns to approach near certainty (see Figure 3.2).

Even with a background in working as a venture capitalist with a decent network, setting up 100+ meetings was not easy. Securing 1,000 "tosses" is impractical. Even if the number of funds isn't finite, your resources to reach 1,000 meaningful meetings is probably finite.

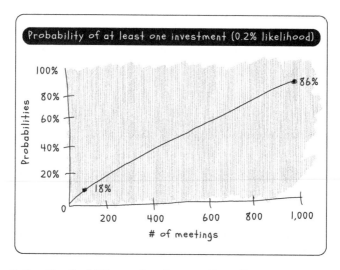

Figure 3.2   Probability of at Least One Investment at 0.2% Chances

Despite the limits, stacking the odds linearly can theoretically increase the probability of my upside to, say, 20% or so at 100 meetings. That's not bad at all. But there is an even better strategy that helped me optimize my upside, which I used for my seed round just five months later. In contrast to the months I spent on my preseed, I closed my seed round within a week with more than $5 million of written commitments by *changing the system*. There are several ways to change the system in your favor, and I'll share two I used directly.

Changing Systems: Order of Operation Unlike a coin toss, where each outcome is independent of the previous toss, investment meetings are dependent on previous outcomes. So, the chances of raising *given* successful commitments in a previous meeting dramatically increase the chances of the next meeting. The magic word *given* hints at conditional probability, which can have counterintuitive statistical results, even for some of the most experienced (there are well-documented experiments of faulty intuition of conditional probability, from the famous Monty Hall problem at MIT involving goats and doors, and Eddy's experiment at Harvard Medical School involving test sensitivity and specificity of breast cancer).

Fundraising, I'd say, is a little more intuitive. Imagine having 100 meetings in place. Say you can secure $100 K from four friends and family members. Securing those by meeting 4 will probably yield far better results than securing the same amount by meeting 96. Having 100% of investors backing a company by meeting number 5 *seems* like a stronger signal than 95% of investors passing on your company by meeting 96. Alluding to the idea of power in negotiation from the earlier section, the earlier you raise the minimal funds to run your company, the more power you'll have in the proceeding meetings, because the less you need the investors. In YC for example, many founders are advised to think of a minimal amount to raise under *cockroach mode* to keep the company alive.

There is a lot at play here. I admit there is some reliance on intuition. But it's hard to prove causal inference anyway. You could dismiss this as reliance on anecdotes or simply faulty psychology of investors, reactively investing from Fear of Missing Out. However, my theory seems to hold in practice in that order of operations matter, especially when founders explain their fundraising process as this domino effect of the first investor leads to a rapid closing of the rest. Even if it is only correlative, simply ordering investors who are most likely to back me earlier dramatically improved my "luck" in realizing my upside scenario. Then there's entirely changing the dynamics of the game.

Changing Systems: Rules of the Game   After the last of my exams at Oxford, I sat in my dorm room, eagerly waiting for the kick-off call to start Y-Combinator. Partners welcomed us novice founders, sharing guidance, many of which were counterintuitive at the time. One pertinent to fundraising was to push all inbound requests from investors toward the end of the three-month accelerator period. On face value, it may seem like a minor detail, but it has noticeable impact.

One rationale was to focus on talking to customers and building the product, rather than be distracted by investors. Another tactical reason was to provide more leverage to founders. Let me explain. Rather than having multiple independent conversations with investors across a long period of time, tightening the investment period with a large number of investors participating simultaneously often shifts the power from investors to founders. It's a minor adjustment to shift some meetings over a few months down the line, but it completely changes the dynamic from a *private sale* to an *open auction*. For those familiar with auction theory, you'll see how under such market dynamics, generally speaking, founders would be at an advantage, assuming the company is functional. Auction theory is a beast of a topic, and for brevity, I'll skip the proofs and models, and share a few intuitive reasons why auctions can be advantageous over a private sale:

- **Parallel Processing:** By speaking to multiple investors simultaneously, the time to raise is significantly reduced from parallel processing the process. Often that means avoiding unnecessary delays on investor diligence and prioritizing the deal over others.
- **Competitive Bidding:** Many investors wanting to invest in my company at the same time (auction) creates competition and urgency rather than private discussion. Investors may yield to more aggressive prices and speed to close the deal.
- **Price Discovery:** Turns out that founders aren't really great at valuing their company, and may undervalue it. Through multiple bidders in the process, it minimizes the chances of undervaluing the company.

Of course, for each of these to be true, formal models would demand far more specification of variables from types of goods, bidder behavior, and market conditions to predict the success of private sales vs. open auctions. But in a practical sense, it is not challenging to see how auction dynamics provide more leverage to founders.

Luck can seem like an uncontrollable variable that explains extraordinary success of many. But optimizations like stacking the odds and changing systems can materially increase your surface area of luck to realize the upside. Over the 10-month period, I managed to raise both a pre-seed and seed round in the order of millions, even rejecting investors who wanted to invest in the company.

Career Swing with Asymmetric Principles

Despite my risk aversion, optimizations allowed me to create a no-loss scenario with a meaningful increase in the probability of realizing my upside. My downside was elevated from a catastrophic pit, all the way to graduating from the University of Oxford. My base case was gaining start-up experience while completing my graduate studies. My upside case, through stacking odds and changing systems, enabled me to be paid to work on solving a problem that will change the world. What seemed like a reckless move to throw away a promising career was a calculated risk that's tolerable even for the most risk averse.

It would be disingenuous of me to attribute the outcome of my career bet solely to *Asymmetric Principles*. Many things went right that were beyond my control. My co-founder turned out to be an exceptionally talented person of character who stuck with me through thick and thin, always keeping in mind of the ground truth, rather than the convenient truth. My first customers gave me a chance by using my product, and many investors, advisors, and mentors were all there to make this happen. Without lessening my gratitude for people who made this happen, it is also true that *Asymmetric Principles* played a big role in making this happen.

As you saw in the example of the book deal, realizing the upside of securing funding raised my possible future outcomes. There is a real path of building a billion-dollar company that truly helps people with this ongoing experiment. You only need a few of the right things for your Super Upside.

Looking Forward

Both examples of 15-minute investments to a book deal and a career swing to raise millions were extremely specific to my situation by design. I wanted to demonstrate exactly how *Asymmetric Principles* can play into life and career decisions to maximize your shot at the Super Upside, while protecting yourself.

By no means is either example some fantastical success—I'm right here with you trying to make it—but it's my way to publicly dogfooding *Asymmetric Principles* applied to my life with skin in the game. These are ongoing experiments that can lead to a best-selling book and a billion-dollar start-up founder or very little. But I do have the conviction to apply these principles in my own life.

Looking forward to Chapter 4, the final chapter of Part I, I'll share why *Asymmetric Principles* isn't just a nice-to-have framework, but a necessary one especially in our times. Taking conventional paths doesn't work anymore.

4

Staying Alive

That's neat, but I'm comfortable living my life. Is this really necessary?

Not long ago, you were probably right. Most of us were all going to be fine. By "us," I mean the vast majority of us living between poverty and an Amex Centurion card. And by "fine," I mean a roof over your head, food on the table, and some occasional joys in your life. However, the threshold to be fine seems to be rising every year. Taking a path of certainty used to mean a stable life with basic comforts. Now, that same certainty means struggling for even the essentials. *Asymmetric Principles* is one playbook to stay alive in the predictably grim paths of traditional systems.

Traditional Systems Don't Work

The risk of not taking any risks, especially in rapidly changing times, has been pointed out in the past. Conan O'Brien put these sentiments in a humorous way in his famed commencement speech for the Dartmouth class of 2011:[1]

> *"Today, you have achieved something special—something only 92 percent of Americans your age will ever know: a college diploma. That's right, with your college diploma you now have a crushing advantage over 8 percent of the workforce. I'm talking about dropout losers like Bill Gates, Steve Jobs, and Mark Zuckerberg."*

A decade after his speech, his prophetic sarcasm now rings truer than ever. College degrees that were once a path to stability do not retain the same value. It seems to take categorically more achievements and productivity to maintain the rapidly deteriorating standard of living. That's just the beginning.

A Roof over Your Head

For many of us early in our careers, having a roof over our heads is now a luxury reserved for the top quintile of the population. Since the financial crash in 2008, the housing price to median income has been rising, and we see it continue to rise. According to Joint Center for Housing Studies of Harvard University, more than 70% of households could afford a home for less than 3× their income until 1994, compared to today where less than 3% can afford it (see Figure 4.1) at that ratio.[2]

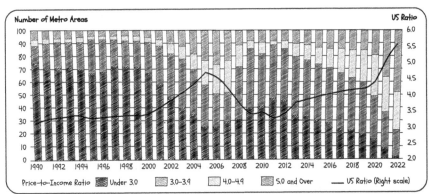

Notes: Price-to-income ratios are for the 100 largest metro areas by population. Home prices are the median sale price of existing single-family homes and incomes are the median household income within markets. Income data for 2022 are based on Moody's Analytics forecasts.
Source: JCHS tabulations of NAR, Metropolitan Median Area Prices; Moody's Analytics estimates.

Figure 4.1   US Metropolitan Home Price to Median Household Income Ratio
Source: Hermann, Alexander, 2024 /https://www.jchs.harvard.edu/blog/home-price-income-ratio-reaches-record-high-0.

In fact, most homes will cost more than 5× the median *household* income, not individual income. When we play this out, here's what this means. Household income in the United States for 2022 is about $74,500[3] according to the US Census Bureau. Even in the most generous assumption of benefiting from zero state taxes and filing jointly, the federal tax and Social Security come to about 15%, bringing after-tax income to about $64,000. Assuming you can spend 25% of your income allocated to a home, it'd take you more than 25 years to eventually pay off the house. Add to that the crazy interest rates on a standard mortgage in 2024, and it can take more than your entire working life to pay it off. This is the best-case scenario for the median household with fantastically generous assumptions. In reality, more than 60% of Americans live paycheck-to-paycheck.[4]

Housing is one of *many* basics needs that continue to grow out of reach for many, especially for younger people. I chose housing for this example because it happens to be the most salient in the minds of people my age. But almost every area that touches the daily lives of everyday people seems to have a bleak outlook from affordability of healthcare to public safety to education. I don't think I need to belabor this point, when we already feel it cut to the bone in our lives. The traditional, stable path doesn't work anymore. Future outlook doesn't look much better, as we face an entire demographic shift, which puts pressure on our social infrastructure. Crumbling has already begun in some parts of the world.

Growing Older, Growing Poorer

Like many immigrant children, I grew up with an identity crisis, looking Korean but feeling Canadian. As a part of a remedy, in 2014, I returned to South Korea for the first time since immigrating to spend a semester at Seoul National University as an exchange student. Reverse culture shock hit me at every turn. Given my appearance and fluency in the language, I was placed under far stricter expectations to adhere to Korean cultures and norms.

But setting aside minor inconveniences, what perplexed me deeply was the state of the elderly people in Korea. I saw many delivering cardboard boxes to recycling depots for their daily sustenance. When I investigated the issue, I learned that almost half of seniors in Korea lived below the relative poverty line (even today, a decade later, that number hovers around 40%).[5] That stat nagged me the entire exchange semester, so much so that I came back the very next year to do something about it. In 2015, I raised money from a large media company to run investigative research and activism related to senior poverty rates. I returned to Seoul National University to do a deep dive on the pension system and social infrastructure for seniors in South Korea. Unfortunately, publishing such politically sensitive content was next to impossible at the time. But I'll share a few findings from my unpublished works, much of which have become common knowledge, almost a decade later, in 2024.

My gut feeling assumed Korea's pension system would be nascent, especially given the economic turmoil just one generation prior. In 1997, Korea was on the cusp of default, barely avoiding collapse with debt restructuring and capital injection from organizations like the International Monetary Fund (IMF).[6] But a minute of research shattered my speculation. Korea boasted the third-largest pension fund in the world—next to Japan and Norway—with 1,000 trillion wons or roughly $760 billion in assets.[7] With so much money, why were so many seniors living in poverty?

At risk of oversimplification, the pension system mimics the mechanics of a lottery or insurance. In principle, *many* people contribute a small premium throughout their life, which funds a large payout to the *few* lucky survivors who live beyond the retirement age. Think of it as an insurance premium. And this worked just fine. When the National Pension System was set up in 1988,[8] average life expectancy was in the mid-1960s,[9] roughly coinciding with the retirement eligibility age of 60.[10] But today, the system is squeezed from both ends with more cash flowing out, and less cash coming in.

Cash outflows increased as the average life expectancy in Korea climbed above 80 by 2010, and only continues to increase according to World Health Organization (WHO) reports.[11] That's like everyone winning the lottery, increasing the total payout from the fund. At the same time, cash inflows are dwindling with fewer people contributing to the pension fund. South Korea hit the lowest Total Fertility Rate (TFR) in the world, with 0.72 in 2023, projected to drop to 0.68 by 2024. For reference, that's far below the rate of 2.1 required to replace the population without immigration.[12]

Obviously, the problem is far hairier than my summary, but roughly speaking, more cash outflow + less cash inflow = depleting fund. Without serious interventions, the pension fund is forecasted to be depleted as early as 2055.[13] For a quick reality check in 2025, the 2050s are just as far away as the 1990s. Korea is not the only country with this problem. Many developed countries are seeing similar effects of varying magnitudes, with increasingly stringent pension eligibility.

Providing for yourself to be "fine" with traditionally stable paths will progressively become harder, not easier. Situations of heading toward a predictable collapse is what start-ups call *default dead*.

Are You Default Dead?

Default dead is a start-up concept—attributed to Paul Graham, the co-founder of Y-Combinator—that refers to a start-up that is very much "alive" today, but will predictably die if nothing changes. For instance, a start-up that continually burns more cash than it generates will predictably run out of money and die. That's default dead. In contrast, when a start-up hits the break-even point—the point when cash in matches cash out—it becomes *default alive*. It's simple arithmetic.

When we consider such a framework for our personal decisions, many of our traditional paths may be *default dead* insofar as affording the essentials to live. Stable paths aren't actually stable anymore, unless by stable you mean predictable, and by predictable, you mean predictably tragic. While I do not want to be the cynic crying that the sky is falling, I urge you not to fall victim to the present bias, and glaze over the situation. Taking the familiar, stable path is probably the riskier path in today's age.

Reassessing the Risk of "Non-Risky" Choices

A year into starting my company, the global economy had a moment of reckoning with the end of ZIRP—Zero Interest Rate Policy. For the tech sector, the era of "free money" was gone, with the gravy train coming to an abrupt halt. Headlines reflected the new reality: traditionally "stable" jobs becoming less than stable with one mass layoff after another. Then there were idiosyncratic events like Elon Musk's infamous 80% cut after acquiring X,[14] formerly Twitter. Since starting my company in 2021, the tech sector in the United States alone laid off 165,000 workers in 2022, 264,000 in 2023, and 134,000 as of August 2024 according to Layoffs.fyi.[15] Even the remaining staff, who weren't directly affected in tech and otherwise, still suffer from mild concerns to fear of being next. That's just in the US tech market, and far worse when played out globally, in combination with macroeconomic factors.

Meanwhile, the "risky" path of starting a company left me with a near-zero chance of getting fired. By staying frugal, we managed to create an 80-month theoretical runway (number of months based on how much we were burning a month relative to how much money we had raised). Of course, this example is purely anecdotal and does not endure statistical scrutiny by any means. However, my point about reassessing the risk of so-called "non-risky" choices stands. There appears to be a growing number of exceptional circumstances and macro factors challenging the stability of traditionally "safe" options—raising the question of whether these exceptions are on the verge of becoming the rule.

The rising threshold to be "fine" coupled with increasingly unreliable traditional paths should be considered as you to play out your personal future scenarios to their predictable conclusions. If you are in fact default dead, then this should serve as a wake-up call to make changes in one way or another.

Becoming Default Alive

Asymmetric Principles happens to be one of the most flexible and powerful ways to flip the switch from default dead to default alive. As you saw in Chapter 3, you can start as small or large as you want. As you apply these principles, you'll start elevating your floor, ending up with continuous sets of no-loss scenarios. Such characteristics of *Asymmetric Principles* make the Super Upside a matter of *when* rather than *if*. Remember that the upsides are so large that you only need a few of these right things to work out for an exceptional outcome, and just one to work out to become default alive. Before diving into Part II of the book for the step-by-step practical guide, I'll share a few positive side effects of *Asymmetric Principles* at play that make the Super Upside a matter of time.

You Compound Luck

Compounding is often used in the context of finance, referring to the process of earning interest on your initial principal, and accumulated interest. As you generate returns, those returns start to generate their own returns, and so on, creating a snowball effect that grows your wealth over time. While it's often used to explain investment returns, it can apply to anything. In fact, one of the central messages of James Clear's famed *Atomic Habits* illustrates a 1% improvement a day leading to a 37-fold improvement over a year.

Continually applying *Asymmetric Principles* compounds luck. I'll share an example of how it played out by closing out my writing example from Chapter 3. A few months into writing on Medium, I hit my base case—developing a modest number of readers who valued my writing. One of my pieces caught the attention of a few Medium employees, and that led to an invitation to be a speaker at Medium's first online conference, which attracted more than 10,000 attendees. I had a chance to speak alongside Olympic athletes, best-selling authors, and Harvard's chair of the Astronomy Department. The commitment was to host four 30-minute talks on a variety of topics from start-ups to career decisions. The cost was about four hours in total: two hours on a Saturday afternoon for the talks, and another two hours to prepare for the sessions, which were mostly adaptations of lectures I'd given in the past. Put another way, the cost was giving up my writing session for the month. Was it worth it? I took a minute to run through the forecasts to assess.

- Base case: Gaining credibility speaking alongside best-selling authors and experts; and generating media assets (the talk would be recorded), which I repurpose on different social platforms in the future.
- Downside case: Wasting time that could've been spent on writing, and perhaps embarrassment if no one shows up to my talks. Both were tolerable downsides for me, given the base case.
- Upside scenario: The base case alone was good enough to push forward, but the upside I sampled was generating potential collaborations with good selection bias in the audience— fellow writers, editors, and creators who may want to work with me in the future. I was playing my odds of finding serendipitous luck.

In the end, I committed to all four sessions. A few days after the talk, I received a LinkedIn message from Christina, an acquisition editor at Wiley. *"Hi Daniel, thank you for contributing to the Medium Day event. Have you considered turning some of those concepts into a book?"* The conversation started in Los Angeles with a few months of negotiation in Tokyo, before finally signing the book deal in Bali.

Recall my first set of scenarios as a writer from Chapter 3. It was not different from anyone starting as an online writer. Reaching my first base case initially led to a speaking opportunity, which came with its own set of scenarios. Reaching my first upside case led to the book deal. In two iterations of *Asymmetric Principles*, my set of future outcomes dramatically improved. My downside is floored at becoming a published author with Wiley and huge possible upsides that are several magnitudes better than when I started. My third and fourth will only raise the quality of possible outcomes even further. With just a few iterations, *Asymmetric Principles* compounds luck, until you hit your Super Upside.

You Attract People Champions

As your luck compounds, you'll start attracting people to champion you. Because the upsides are so large, applying *Asymmetric Principles* often creates a positive bias for people to prioritize their resources and invest in you. To borrow a framework from Adam Grant's book, *Give and Take*, there are three archetypes of people in terms of reciprocal behavior:

- Givers, who give more than they receive
- Matchers, who balance what they give and what they take
- Takers, who take more than they give

There is considerable nuance I'm leaving out here (a giver in social context may be a matcher in business context, for example), but these are roughly the archetypes. Givers will naturally be inclined to help, but *Asymmetric Principles* really gives you an edge with Matchers and Takers.

Even the Takers Will Champion You   All of us, at some point or another, have been on the receiving end of givers, who generously extended a lending hand without demanding something in return. I certainly have received such kindness. I've also traded in a chip or two with matchers in the work place. Then there are takers. In my view, takers shouldn't be demonized, especially in the context of the workplace, where they are simply prioritizing the interests of themselves and their loved ones. You've probably periodically received emails from strangers who ask to "pick your brain" or "learn more." These requests only increase over time. Maybe you're willing to take those 15 minutes out of your day but let's play out this scenario to its limit. You have 24 hours in a day. Maybe the first few times you feel flattered that someone is seeking your advice. But what if it grows to 10 people a day? That's 3 hours. With 32 people asking for a coffee, your entire workday would be gone. At a certain point, people have to prioritize their time, money, and brain space. You do too. Imagine ignoring one of the 100 daily requests, and then a rumor circulates that you're a greedy, calculating capitalist who only hangs out with hot shots, and sees people as objects. It's probably not a fair characterization of who you are or takers.

But even if you're less than generous with your view of takers, *Asymmetric Principles* will often convince them to play ball, and prioritize you. Asymmetric upsides, by definition, are phenomenally large. You're swinging for a home run. Even if you're personally a giver or matcher, put yourself in the shoes of takers. If a taker had 15 minutes to invest in someone, which would be more attractive? Someone who asks for your help to be promoted 3 months faster or someone who asks for your help with a clear, non-zero shot at building the next Google or curing chronic conditions like diabetes and hair loss? People are attracted to being a part of big outcomes that matter.

Skin in the Game   Once you win over the givers, matchers, and takers, they now have a vested interest in your success. This is a simple enough intuition. For those of you who have done matchmaking among your friends, you want that couple to succeed. Or if you've ever referred someone to your company, you want that person to do well, maybe for that referral bonus, but more importantly for your own reputation.

Beyond intuitions, there are real psychological effects at play like the desire to avoid cognitive dissonance. Posited by psychologist Leon Festiner, it refers to the mental discomfort that comes from holding conflicting beliefs at the same time. People invested their time and energy in your work. Why would they invest their time in something that isn't successful? That'd be uncomfortable. It has to be a success. And when you do eventually realize the upside, everyone benefits.

You Build Resilience to Failure

The last positive side effect I'll mention is resilience to failure. When you work out the nature of *Asymmetric Principles*, you'll know that 90% of your shots will fail, and that's by design. That works, because you know you just need a few of these to hit the upside. Understanding that principle can go a long way in building grit, at any stage, which helped me in earlier parts of my life.

Going to college wasn't an obvious option open to me. I wasn't sure if I'd be able to afford it. Starting my last year of high school, I applied for more than 120 scholarships over four years. My expectation was not winning 100% of the applications. I just needed a few to turn out. Ultimately, 20 generous foundations funded my tuition, living expenses, and then some extra to support my family financially during my studies.

Writing those 120 applications was a grind, coming out to about a quarter-million words—the equivalent to four books in length. Every rejection stung; but understanding the probabilities and knowing I only needed a few right things in *Asymmetric Principles* helped me keep going for four years. It's what Angela Duckworth, psychologist at the University of Pennsylvania, may describe as *grit*: "Holding steadfast to that goal. Even when you fall down. Even when you screw up. Even when progress toward that goal is halting or slow," which she describes as a key indicator of success.

Following a traditionally stable path may unintentionally lock you into a default dead trajectory. *Asymmetric Principles*, at the very least, forces you to work out predictable outcomes and clarify where you stand. In my view, *Asymmetric Principles* is one of the best frameworks to tip you over to becoming default alive and maximize luck for outsized outcomes. Positive byproducts like compounding luck, attracting champions, and bolstering resilience only accelerate the timeline to reach your Super Upside.

Why Now?

At the risk of sounding like a cynic, the outcomes of most traditional paths are becoming predictably bad. The threshold of being "fine" through established routes has narrowed, now reserved only for those at the top of that particular game. The risk of taking no-risk is growing, quietly pushing people into predictably default dead ends. Today, more than ever, outsized returns aren't just nice-to-haves—they're necessities. *Asymmetric Principles* is a playbook designed to help almost anyone to structurally place themselves in the path of luck, reaching the Super Upside while protecting themselves.

In Part I of this book, concluding with this chapter, I laid out the theoretical foundations upon which the following chapter will build. Extraordinary outcomes are less about a perfect score and more about a few right things. Some of the most successful industries and careers are built on the few right asymmetric bets— outsized upsides that dwarf the cost and the risk of the opportunity—that enable success despite being *wrong most of the time*. Building on frameworks (like scenario forecasts and *Need-to-Believe)* through personal experiments, I introduced qualifiers to apply these principles to life decisions: upside case with a clear, non-zero probability path to a large, uncapped rapid growth; base case that brings you where you want to go; and downside case that is floored, tolerable, and predictable. Super Upsides matter more than ever, as traditional paths are increasingly leading to predictably bad outcomes.

Taken together, Part I provides the building blocks of *Asymmetric Principles*. In Part II, I'll build on the foundations of Part I and provide a detailed step-by-step guide to help you start applying *Asymmetric Principles* in your own life.

PART

II

The Practical Guide

In Part II, I'll shift the style of the book from theory to practice. The next four chapters will feel like a set of case studies and exercises, and less like passive food for thought like Part I. The chapters are dense, since they serve as a practical guide on applying *Asymmetric Principles* from the very first stage of finding the right opportunities all the way to realizing your Super Upside:

- Chapter 5 introduces the base language of *systems*, which will be the level of analysis when applying *Asymmetric Principles*. Different types of systems will be introduced, starting with one to identify and optimize asymmetric opportunities while avoiding Type I and Type II errors. Competing on the best systems, not analysis, is what will maximize our luck of the Super Upside.
- Chapter 6 shares a set of systems for the earliest stages of *Asymmetric Principles*. It's a step-by-step guide to realize the first set of upsides in your life. Taking the theory of start-ups as a foundation, I adapt critical components for *Asymmetric Principles*, which boils down to good hypotheses and good experiments.
- Chapter 7 first discusses structural limits of systems and conveys the need to adopt new systems to keep momentum. Following, I dissect systems of leverage designed to scale early signs of success to the Super Upside.

- In Chapter 8, I discuss how intentional portfolio construction of systems can work together to diversify risk of any single system and work together to elevate the entire portfolio. More importantly, I consider how *Asymmetric Principles* fits in with the rest of your life in a "life portfolio."

The practical guide serves as a starting point across every stage of *Asymmetric Principles* and should continue to be a reference point as you move upward toward your Super Upside.

5

Choosing the Right Games to Play

"People think focus means saying yes to the thing you've got to focus on. But that's not what it means at all. It means saying no to the hundred other good ideas that there are. . . . Innovation is saying no to 1,000 things."

—Steve Jobs[1]

What you don't want to do after reading the first four chapters of this book is to immediately take every life decision and forecast scenarios. If you did try, you'll quickly find out it's not feasible in practice. Application of *Asymmetric Principles* works on levels of *systems* rather than individual analysis. In fact, every stage of *Asymmetric Principles* requires a different system, and intuitively so— optimal systems to start a company are different from scaling it to eight figures. Similarly, optimizations for early stages of *Asymmetric Principles* of identifying the few right things and generating initial traction will be different from later stages of scaling with leverage and building portfolios of asymmetric opportunities.

This chapter will scope the definitions and boundaries of systems for the purposes of this book. The purpose is for precision in future discussion of systems, especially choosing and optimizing the right systems for each stage of the *Asymmetric Principles* journey. The predictor of success will be driven by who adopts and executes on a superior system.

Taking a Page from Investors

Admittedly, I left out a few important details in Chapter 1 for dramatic effect. While it's true that venture investors only need a small hit rate for massive outcomes, the hit rate excludes thousands of companies they *didn't* invest in. Good investors are judged on both their hit rates and their miss rates. For any given investment opportunity, there are two axes of decisions each with binary outcomes. The first one is held by the investor, who decides to either invest in or pass on a company. The second is held by the company, delivering success or failing within a certain time frame (the investor can always invest in later stages). The combination of outcomes can be summarized in a four-by-four matrix (see Figure 5.1).

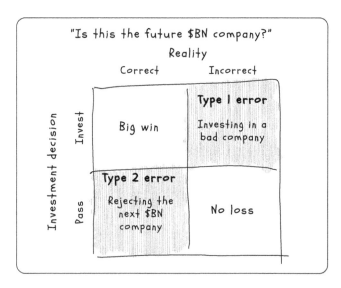

Figure 5.1   Type I and Type II Errors in Venture Investing

For an investor, the best-case scenario is choosing to invest in a company that ends up being successful—the top left quadrant of Figure 5.1. The second-best scenario—the bottom right quadrant—is passing on a company that ends up failing. The remaining two scenarios—the top right and bottom left quadrants—are the errors investors want to avoid. These are called Type I and Type II errors:

- **Type I error** is investing in a company that ends up failing. That is the primary error I discussed in the first four chapters.
- **Type II error** is passing on a company that ends up being successful. Imagine passing on investing in the early days of Apple or NVIDIA.

Investors minimize both Type I and II errors while balancing their resources and time to make the best decisions.

Systems to Reject Distractions

Early-stage venture capitalists invest in about 0.2% of the companies they come across, or roughly 1 in 500 investments. Typically, an average seed-stage venture fund invests in 10 to 15 companies per year. If we scale these rates linearly, a fund will need to evaluate 5,000 companies to find 10 investments for the year.

Assuming 260 working days, that's 19 companies per day. Spending equal amount of time on every due diligence process—that takes anywhere from a week to several months—would be impossible. To solve this problem, every investor I know has a system to get to a "no" quickly—sometimes from an email headline—to focus their time on the right opportunities. It ends up looking like a funnel, with an illustrative example below:

- 1 minute: Pre-qualification—Does it hit minimal requirements?
- 5–10 minutes: Research—Do I understand what it is, and do I like it?

- 1 Hour: Assessment—If everything the company says is true, and my understanding of the market is true, do I have conviction to invest?
- Days: Due diligence—Was everything indeed true? Do I still have conviction with new information?

These systems are often called *scoping*, which is necessary to make quality, high-volume decisions. Scoping doesn't need to be grandiose. Some are as simple and arbitrary as disqualifying industries (gambling, cannabis) or companies selling to consumers. But the point is that investors use **systems** to incrementally spend more time on a narrower set of opportunities. They want to spend as much time as possible discerning between great to excellent companies. So the greater the quality of the pool, the better the chances of actually generating 100× returns, which is the primary goal of investors. Order of operations matter. Investors compete more on the systems that can consistently generate the correct decisions—in this case, decisions to choose which companies are worth their time—and less on having a marginally better analysis of a single company. Analysis comes after. To be clear, better systems don't always lead to better outcomes. But it increases the average probability of hitting the Super Upside.

Not unlike investors, we also make thousands of decisions with limited resources. It is impractical to waste brain space on the "nonasymmetric" decisions. The game we're playing is crafting the best systems to optimize all decisions without our direct attention, and then concentrating on the few that matter.

Systems, Not Analysis

According to literature of decision-making, people make, on average, around 30,000 to 35,000 decisions per day.[2] Those decisions include anything from minor decisions like the toppings on your Starbucks coffee to consequential ones like choosing a life partner. Imagine two systems, where one system consistently exercises 1% superior judgment than the other. At the rate of 30,000 decisions a day, the impact of good and bad systems compound significantly in a short period of time. For a reference point, we've discussed that Clear's *Atomic Habits* relies precisely on the compounding effects that drive the 1% daily improvement leading to a 37 times improvement over the course of that year.[3] Now imagine the compounding effects of a system that exercises 1% better judgment on *30,000* decisions daily. It is terrifying to me that the foundational model that powers our decision-making systems between lunch specials often is the same one that powers momentous decisions in our lives.

We All Use Systems—It's a Matter of Which One

At such high volumes of decisions, taking even a single second per decision would be a full-time job. So how do we solve this mathematical problem? Unfortunately, we have no option but to rely on a system of some sort, even if it's a horrible one. As Yale psychology professor Paul Bloom shared in his 2009 freshman lecture:[4]

> *"It turns out that collecting information about categories is essential to our survival. . . . So, when you see this object over here you categorize it as a chair and you recognize that you could probably sit on it. . . . These are all stereotypes about chairs and about apples and about dogs. It doesn't mean they're logically true. This could be a vegetarian dog, a poison apple, an explosive chair, but they're typically true. And if you were suddenly stripped of your ability to make generalizations, you'd be at a loss."*

The word *system* can imply some level of sophistication, but it's your brain saying, "Well, that sort of worked before in a similar case, and I didn't hate what happened. Let's do it again." Rather than individually analyzing every decision, this "sort of worked" decision model is used as the base system until it leads to a horrible, memorable, and often immediate, outcome. It's rudimentary pattern recognition that processes decisions meeting an acceptable, *satisfactory* level that differs for everyone.

This base model of the brain isn't my conjecture, but one posited by Herbert Simon, often considered the precursor to modern behavioral economics. In his award-winning findings from the Royal Swedish Academy of Sciences, he formalized the types of systems we employ. It uses simple rules based on experiences that lead to what he called *satisficing*[5] or "good enough" outcomes, contrary to the standard economic model of maximizers. But whether you're maximizing, satisficing, or minimizing, the take-home point is that we are all *already using systems*. It's simply a matter of *which* systems we use to make decisions, each with trade-offs. There are no other ways to feasibly solve the computational limitations of our mind. Unfortunately, our natural systems are less than optimal for identifying asymmetric opportunities.

Our Natural Systems Are Faulty

In 2012, I was knee-deep into behavioral economics for no obvious benefit other than satisfying my own curiosity. I read every behavioral economics book published at the time, mistakenly thinking I was an "expert" on the topic. With the brashness of a freshman, I found myself debating my professor in my introductory class. It was an elementary point about challenging the predictability of "known" heuristics—mental shortcuts people use to make decisions—that predictably seems to fall under different types of stressors (uncomfortable discussion with a mother-in-law vs. digesting bad news at work). Or at least that some people seem to have better heuristics (or systems) than others in different forms of stress.

Instead of refuting point by point, Professor Peter Younkin responded with amusement and offered me a job on the spot. That job was supporting his research in investor behavior in choosing between thousands of crowdfunding projects. How did investors choose which ones to evaluate, and what drove their decisions to eventually invest? In those short two years, I saw just how impressively creative people can be in making faulty decisions, which relates directly to finding the few right things.

Of course, the essence of this book is not to summarize every human bias in decision-making, but practically applying *Asymmetric Principles*. For pertinence, I'll focus on why our natural systems have horrible intuition to identify the few right things—particularly processing outsized outcomes—which are critical to *Asymmetric Principles*.

Wrong Intuition of Asymmetric Outcomes   Take a look at the line in Figure 5.2. Where would you place the number 1,000,000?

In one study, about half of adult Americans placed it roughly halfway between the thousand and billion "as though they believe that the number words 'thousand, million, billion, trillion' constitute a uniformly spaced count list."[6]

These results are not unexpected. Methods of the brain processing numerical information through spatial representation were discovered as early as the late 1800s from the likes of Francis Galton with a "mental imagery" discovery[7] and Jean Piaget in his work with children and their interaction with numbers.[8] One of the contributors who advanced the understanding of the shape of such spatial representation is the French cognitive neuroscientist Stanislas Dehaene.

Dehaene hypothesized that people didn't process numbers in isolation, but they instead mapped numbers onto an internal spatial model, which he called the *mental number line*. The concept posits that people visualize numbers spatially with small numbers positioned to the left, and larger numbers to the right. Even here, there is a difference in

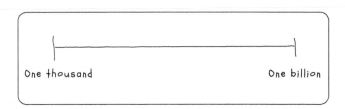

Figure 5.2   Line Between One Thousand and One Billion

interpreting numbers as Arabic numerals (1) or words (one). To investigate the shape and properties of the number line, Dehaene conducted an experiment where research participants were presented with pairs of numbers—say 2 and 9—and asked to identify which was larger. By measuring the response times for pairs of numbers with different relative proximities, Dehaene tried to reverse-engineer the brain's processing of numbers by size.

One key finding was the mental spacing between smaller and larger numbers. For example, the response time to identify the larger number for the pair 1 and 2 was faster than 98 and 99. Plotting the spacing based on latency, the larger numbers were compressed, creating a shape that took the form of a logarithmic model.[9] And this finding seems to be a universal instinct across cultures.[10]

Graphically, logarithmic curve is the *exact inverse* of exponential curve, which happens to be how Super Upsides are realized in exponential growth. This is just one example of how our natural systems can be a detriment to working with *Asymmetric Principles*. These may seem like minor concerns that can be manually addressed, but effects of systems compound on too many decisions.

Quality of Systems Compound

Imagine even the smallest of these flaws compounding the 30,000 decisions in your life. Left unattended, these systems can be easily manipulated to bring out catastrophic decisions and outcomes, certainly in our own lives, but in the lives of others. Controversial experiments like the Milgram's Obedience Experiment which convinced people it's okay to kill people with a lab coat[11] and the Stanford Prison Experiment that had students abusing each other with a little role play[12]—I'm being simplistic here—demonstrated just how fragile decision-making systems can be. A few tricks here and there on the decision-making system were enough to persuade people it's okay to abuse and even kill people. I share this example to show that the solution here is not to relegate imperfect systems entirely as "bad," and pretend to analyze every decision instead. As we've discussed, this is not possible. We all adapt some system at some point to live our lives, so the solution lies in choosing and improving the right systems. For example, combatting stereotypes won't work by pretending to assess every individual and aspect of life from ground zero. It would be willful ignorance to pretend this is possible. Instead, we need to embrace the idea that systems are necessary and attempt to create better systems for decision-making, and that includes systems favorable for *Asymmetric Principles*.

Improving Systems

But all is not lost. Our systems turn out to be quite malleable. There are at least two ways to improve systems to work in your favor to consistently improve decision-making: deliberation and recalibration.

Designing Systems Through Deliberation

Deliberation, in short, is understanding where the faults of systems lie, and addressing them ahead of time to ensure that optimal decisions are made.

Nir Eyal, in his book *Indistractable*, shares practical insights to staying focused on what matters—what you deem "to matter" anyway. In his words, "You can't call something a distraction unless you know what it is distracting you from."[13] In Eyal's view, anything that brings you toward your desire is traction. Everything else is a distraction. The strategy of *pre-commitments*—similar to the Ulysses pact from Chapter 2—is one that keeps us from making predictable errors. He posits that a primary source of distraction is discomfort, and we resort to easier tasks that seem productive, like checking emails. By understanding where our systems fall short, we can influence future decision-making. For example, by increasing the impulse to check our phone by turning it off and leaving it in a different room, it reduces the frequency of that action.

Professor Paul Bloom echoes such strategies that shape our systems. In his 2014 TED talk, Bloom shared a polemic case that systems like generalizations and stereotypes are in fact not "a child of ignorance"—that is, not just a lack of knowledge—but can be rational. By rational, he means that they are necessary to survive. Bloom acknowledges both the necessity and flaws of such systems, and follows up with a prescription on how to minimize its dangers, and it's by *binding ourselves* through deliberation.[14] An example he shares is adopting a blind audition system in orchestras to eliminate biases that we know probably exist in our decision-making systems. In essence, it's a way to frontload to exploit errors in your systems so you don't have to rethink and reanalyze every time with reasonable assurance of making the right call.

Designing Systems Through Recalibration

The second way to improve systems is recalibration, which entirely changes the intuitions of our systems. Our systems are not set in stone. Daniel Kahneman and Amos Tversky, pioneers of behavioral economics, advanced and formalized the concepts of Herbert Simon into Prospect Theory, which earned them the coveted Nobel Prize in Economics.[15] Kahneman and Tversky summarized their findings in their book *Thinking Fast and Slow*, which discusses a core concept by distinguishing between two systems of thinking:

- **System 1:** The fast system, which handles high-volume decisions through rules that favor speed over optimization, which are called heuristics.
- **System 2:** The slow system, which deliberates on optimizing rather than processing volume.

In other words, we can use decision-making systems we control to recalibrate the core decision-making system. As Kahneman puts it, "System 2 has some ability to change the way System 1 works, by programming it to follow a rule or by setting up particular intentions and expectations."[16]

Our natural systems are not fixed and can be recalibrated to set new instincts. When I first started my company, my initial intuition was to protect my start-up idea behind an NDA (nondisclosure agreement) in case someone steals it. After a few years in evaluating early-stage companies and pitching my own company, I realized that everyone is so busy with their own ideas, and start-ups have so much execution risk, I opened it up and got as much help as I could. My "System 2," so to speak, established a pattern to share my ideas openly, which over time were internalized as instincts. Similarly with fundraising, my intuition was to raise as much as I could on the highest possible valuation, which shifted to avoiding arbitrarily high valuations decoupled from the performance of my company. These decisions become an immediate response. Recently, I burned my thumb on a hot plate. The intense pain from the blister concerned me. But a trained doctor constantly exposed to burn injuries would probably be alarmed more by the absence of pain, as it could indicate nerve damage from a deeper burn. You can probably think of your own examples of counterintuitive truths that have been recalibrated as an instinct for you.

To ground these anecdotes with objectivity, I'll share Robert Siegler's research, which also closes out the mental number line experiments. Building on the works of Herbert Simon, Siegler discovered that natural spatial representation of numbers can change. Through his work in cognitive development and reasoning in children, he found education and exposure to mathematics can shift the mental number line from a logarithmic one to a linear one. The refined understanding and continued exposure to numbers aligned the mental model with reality, where each unit increase represents the same amount of numerical difference, without arbitrary compression of spaces for large numbers.[17]

Recalibration Implies Errors   One of the most impressive recalibrations I've seen comes from Ray Dalio. Dalio is the founder of Bridgewater Associates, the largest actively managed hedge fund in the world, with more than $120 billion as of August 2024.[18] In his book *Principles*, he describes a complex mental model of the world economy with billions of dollars behind the conviction in that model.[19] That system is the basis for investment decisions at one of the most successful hedge funds in the world.

The purpose of recalibrating your systems is not to never be wrong, but to continue to improve your systems for making better decisions over time. This may sound suspiciously similar to the satisficing system that uses basic trial and error. But the core difference is that we can pinpoint *exactly* where our system failed, which enables continual improvement. For example, Dalio discusses his crippling failure of 1982 debt crisis management that nearly killed his company. His system failed. That led to him studying in depth the behaviors of debt cycles, which he details in his book. He not only looked at the present variables, but he studied all financial crises throughout history as a way to improve his principles. These updates were incorporated into investment principles— I imagine with deliberation—and over time became internalized as instincts. That led to a much more controlled loss for Bridgewater during the financial crisis of 2008. This iterative process echoes Dalio's principles of "Pain + Reflection = Progress." The core aspect is, of course, reflection, and using what comes of that reflection to update your systems to make a better set of decisions.

Systems for Asymmetric Principles

This chapter introduced the necessary context of systems, which will be the level of analysis to apply *Asymmetric Principles*. Everyone uses systems. It's just a matter of which system. New systems can be adopted, and existing systems recalibrated to better fit your objectives over time. Even minor difference in systems can have dramatic compounding effects in your life.

Interestingly, despite its shortfalls, our base natural *satisficing system* tends to work for most things in life, most of the time. But *Asymmetric Principles* is entirely a game of outliers. Its defining characteristic is the *exceptional* outcome. *Asymmetric Principles* demands specific systems to optimize your chances of the Super Upsides. Chapter 6 will introduce the first of many systems used to apply *Asymmetric Principles*, starting with identifying the few right things and securing your very first upsides: through good hypotheses and good experiments.

6 | Everything Is a Hypothesis

If you double the number of experiments you do per year, you're going to double your inventiveness.[1]

—Jeff Bezos

There is value in taking time to consider which set of systems to use and adapt. Every system has trade-offs, better positioned for some things and not others. While there are superior systems that may dominate inferior systems, systems of similar quality will come down to the use of the most appropriate one. Moreover, adopting new systems and fine-tuning your existing systems take considerable time, and even more so to reap the compounded benefits. Be mindful of the systems you adopt. Chapter 6 introduces the system designed to optimize the probability of securing your very first upsides.

Theory of Start-ups as the Foundational System

By far the best system to start applying *Asymmetric Principles* is one I've learned as a start-up founder, loosely known as the theory of start-ups. The theory of start-ups is a collection of coinciding insights and observed patterns from the titans of the industry. That includes *Zero to One* by Peter Thiel, founder of PayPal; *The Hard Thing About Hard Things* by Ben Horowitz, co-founder of Andreessen Horowitz; *Build* by Tony Fadell, builder of the iPhone; *The Lean Startup* by Eric Ries, co-founder of IMVU and LSTE; *The Mom Test* by Rob Fitzpatrick; *Hooked* by Nir Eyal; a collection of essays by Paul Graham, co-founder of Y-Combinator; and many others who have formally and informally contributed to this collection. Together they've come up with several frameworks that tend to maximize success of early-stage start-ups, many of which I've used actively in my own journey of starting a company. If you had to boil down a founder's primary role, it's the speed of exercising good judgment, even in the absence of complete information and abundant resources—exactly what you'll need in the early days of applying *Asymmetric Principles*. There are at least two other structural reasons why aspects of theory of start-ups are highly applicable for realizing your first few upsides: proven structure and accountable feedback.

Proven Structure

Theory of start-ups converged from mass experimentation of thousands of entrepreneurs going from zero to one—or finding their initial traction—with constrained resources and attention. The approach helps founders continuously hyperfocus on the right games to play and consistently realize the asymmetric upsides—both essential for an early-stage start-up to survive.

At any given moment, there are a hundred things fighting for my attention in my start-up. Investors, accountants, lawyers, customers, and everyone else tells me their problem is the most urgent and material. Theory of start-ups helps founders relentlessly prioritize the few right things with outsized returns to drive the company forward. But it doesn't stop there. Founders have to pull off asymmetric upsides consistently in these few right things. Recall in Chapter 3, the example of raising capital with exceptionally low odds that required considerable work including optimizations like linear stacking of luck and changing systems. That's one of many asymmetric upsides required to keep my start-up alive. Founders then must build and distribute products people want, which few start-ups ever do. Founders must raise funding across several rounds, which few start-ups manage to do. Founders must build a world-class team and scale with culture, which few start-ups manage to do. And so on. Theory of start-ups has become a proven structure to help founders consistently focus on the right things and generate outsized returns in the early days.

Accountable Feedback

These frameworks aren't intellectual exercises from a vacuum. They are a collection of observations, insights, and patterns culminated by investors and entrepreneurs who have considerable skin in the game. Investors risk millions on the outcome of the start-up, and founders often bet their entire life on their companies. The stakes are simply too high for catchy, idealistic approaches. Instead, theory of start-ups has actionable principles, open to change from immediate feedback loops—I feel like I get punched in the face every day—carried out by thousands of entrepreneurs finding their path to their outsized wins. Wrong decisions or even slow decisions can lead to the death of the company. As a general rule, frameworks removed from practice tend to lose touch with reality. Nassim Nicholas Taleb echoes this sentiment in his book *Skin in the Game*, sharing that guidance with skin in the game has the highest probability of being correct.[2]

While this chapter will not cover the entirety of the theory of start-ups, it will borrow aspects that identify asymmetric opportunities and consistently maximize the probabilities of realizing upsides. Ultimately, that comes down to good hypotheses and good experiments.

Good Hypotheses = Good Starting Point

Lying flat on my bed in my dorm room at Oxford, my mind was racing with an endless number of start-up ideas. Should I build a market to rent out inventory in car dealerships? What about an app to coordinate parties with my friends? Or an AI therapist for mental health with everyone stuck at home? Or maybe a product to aggregate all my credit card, hotel, and airline points in one place. Similarly, you may be stuck in the perpetual loops of "What ifs" in your own life, between getting a job, creating a TikTok account, making music, starting an e-commerce store, going to grad school, doing a bootcamp, writing a newsletter, starting a family, moving cities, and any endless number of things you could do.

Choosing a good problem, and eventually a good idea—the one with the maximum chances of becoming a billion-dollar company—is one of the first things a founder has to nail. For you, the question is to maximize your chances of the Super Upside. The challenge is to pick the few right things among hundreds out there. In fact, it's such an important topic that several books have been dedicated on prescriptions to find and evaluate ideas, from "solve a problem for yourself" to "use your unfair advantage" to "painkillers, not vitamins."

Roughly, these prescriptions suggest that a good idea comes from a set of probable hypotheses that, if proven correct in your favor, would lead to your desired outcome. Once that analysis is done, then it's considered a good starting point to start running experiments against the real world. When your hypotheses are proven to line up in the real word, you realize your upside. That good starting point helps you reject the 99 other things to focus on the few right things. One approach I'll share to find your good starting point is by screening by (1) Reasons to Reject; (2) Reasons to Win; (3) Reasons to Invest.

Reasons to Reject: Scoping

For venture capital math to work, the winner needs to be outsized to cover all losses. That means every investment needs to have a probability of generating that 100× return. Otherwise, it would fall outside of the scope. Founders have to make a similar bet, but the stakes are infinitely higher. The company is not one of many, but the only one for the founders. Just as investors and founders require outsized returns as a definitional scope, your initial kill criterion will start with the following question:

- Does this opportunity have the components of *Asymmetric Principles*?
- In Chapter 2, I introduced the definitional characteristics of *Asymmetric Principles*; I've shared a summary in Table 6.1 as a refresher.

Table 6.1   Summary of Asymmetric Principles

Scenarios	Characteristics
• Upside	• Disproportionately outsizes both the investment and all other ranges of scenarios
	• Non-zero, visible path to realize the upside (Need-to-Believe)
	• Uncapped, without artificial barriers
• Base case	• Takes you where you want to go
• Downside	• Outcomes are predictable
	• Outcomes are tolerable
	• Outcomes are floored

Understanding optimization may be needed, set up rough forecasts to screen opportunities by these definitional characteristics. By the way, your first set of forecasts and upside need not be monumental. *Asymmetric Principles* was intentionally designed so anyone can get started without specific degrees, experiences, or backgrounds. In that spirit, I'll share a less than perfect example of how I applied *incomplete,* but nonetheless, some components of the principles when I had nothing.

No money. No network. No reputation.

From Ground Zero   I grew up in a small Canadian town with a population of about 3,000 people—a type of place where the smell of animal manure lingered everywhere. When high school graduation came around, I only had enough money to pay for two college application fees. As much as college is criticized, access to a college education was important to me, because it was one of the few doors that could open opportunities. I had two bullets in my chamber to make the right call.

With an allergic reaction to risks, I used my first shot to secure an early admission to my local college that came with a full ride scholarship. In hindsight, making that call provided a predictable, floored, tolerable downside of a college education. With my remaining shot, I applied to McGill University in Montreal. My offer came with a few scholarships, which would cover my tuition, but not enough to cover living expenses or support my family financially.

Let's call my upside attending McGill without being financially crushed. Scoping that comes into play is how to invest the tight resources to get there. Of the half-dozen options I had at the time, my immediate instinct was to start working part time. My friends worked part time, and I could ask for referrals and work day shifts between classes, and work night shifts in the evening. Starting now would give me the best chances of securing more hours and raise hourly rates with promotions in the future. It was a strategy with concrete actions. Sounds great, right?

Then I did some quick math—a much rustier version of the Need-to-Believe analysis. My initial calculations required about another $120,000 over four years to cover my tuition and living expenses, while continuing to support my family. It turns out, I'd have to work part-time jobs for a very long time to afford it. Even if all probable upside cases of securing shifts, overtime, and promotions occurred, I would not reach my upside. Contrary to my instinct, working part-time jobs would detract me from the upside, which definitionally doesn't meet *Asymmetric Principles*. This is an example of how ignoring the details can lead to pitfalls. I'll digress briefly, as this is a crucial enough point.

The Angel Is in the Details At the outset of this chapter, I mentioned that any system takes time to adopt. The first few times of running through the scenario forecasts of a decision, and now scoping, will feel painfully slow. It may even feel like a waste of time. That's normal. It takes time to recalibrate systems before it becomes an instinct.

Resist the temptations to skip steps or ignore details for speed. Every qualifier from the Need-to-Believe analysis to floored downside in your forecasts exists for a reason, and deviating should come with recognition that it may be outside the scope of *Asymmetric Principles*. These qualifiers are designed to protect you from common pitfalls, which I'll share below:

- **Illusion of progress.** The mistake is equating action with progress. Desire to do something in the midst of anxiety even if the upside has no way of being realized and the base case detracts you from where you want to go. It's similar to the urge to take a detour on a highway even if waiting in traffic is faster. That's the pitfall I would've fallen into had I spent all my time securing part-time jobs and shifts: working hard, yet drifting further away from my goals. Running the Need-to-Believe analysis can minimize this risk.

- **Addiction to potential without doing the work.** Being in a state of potential for a massive upside can be addictive. But without a clear, non-zero path it's not much different than gambling—a state of anticipation, but betting your time instead of money. The worst part is that you can feel like the hero, and congratulate yourself for grit and resilience, hoping to prove people wrong one day. Setting a base case that takes you where you want to go reduces this risk.

- **Uncalculated risk.** Taking a swing with catastrophic downsides would have symmetrical ups and downs—not asymmetrical. I've seen people suddenly wanting to take impulsive risks after years of playing it safe, at times, driven by an identity crisis. Flooring the downsides keeps the asymmetry.

- **All or nothing fallacy.** This is the opposite problem from the above pitfalls: ruling out decisions by overestimating risk. Chapter 10 will discuss this in detail, but this takes the form of thinking that your decision is permanent without an exit or "revolving door." For example, it's overestimating the downside of a PhD program as five years wasted without considering that you can drop out after a few weeks if you hate it. Precisely walking through the downside avoids ruling out good options.

These pitfalls are, by no means, comprehensive, but they demonstrate how lack of detail can lead to bad outcomes, which can be avoided with qualifiers. Investing the time to take the whole system will protect you, and strengthen convictions in your decisions, avoiding questions on your decisions every time your feelings (and instincts) run contrary to the decision. That's counterproductive. Systems are set in place precisely because you want to make reliable decisions despite your cognitive biases, faulty intuitions, and emotions.

In the case of my example from college, I worked backward from the goal that I had in mind to then run rough scenario forecasts to eliminate options that detracted me from that goal. If the first part of scoping was finding reasons to reject an opportunity that did not definitively meet the criteria of *Asymmetric Principles*, the next part of scoping is to find reasons to accept an opportunity. Put another way, the "reason to reject" scoping generates a pool of highly probable asymmetric opportunities, and the "reason to win" prioritizes opportunities within that pool.

Reasons to Win: Unfair Advantages

Investors call these reasons to win an unfair advantage or in the theory of start-ups, founder-market-fit, which suggests that founders should have some competitive background to work on a particular idea. What advantage do founders have in building that billion-dollar company over everyone else who could do this? For example, if you're building an accounting software, hopefully you know something about accounting or software. These unfair advantages can come in the form of your background, your expertise, your access, your location, your skills, and whatever else that biases you toward realizing the upside.

When I say, "whatever else," I truly mean that, as long as it's an edge that will allow you to win. The founders of Service Titan, for example, grew up with immigrant parents who were working in trade, and had exposure into the problems and workflows that come with managing a trades business.[3] In college, the founders used software to streamline the "operating system" for the trades, and eventually reached an $8.3 billion valuation.[4] That's not to say their early exposure from their parents' work was responsible for generating such an outcome, but it was one form of many unfair advantages. That unfair advantage was another reason I was adamant about scholarships ahead of college.

My First Upside   With part-time work ruled out, did I manage to go to McGill? In the end, I allocated all my spare time to applying to scholarships and bursaries. From a scenario perspective, my upside case was winning enough scholarships to be a full-time student while I supported my family. Scholarships that came with the offer would fund my first year. So my base case was taking a few semesters off to work, allowing me to cover my living expenses and support my family—taking about six years to graduate. And I had already floored my downside, which was going to my local college. As you've seen from Chapter 2, I realized my very first upsides, which became the foundation to my career.

Investing all my time in scholarships was not the intuitive move. Eliminating paths like part-time work and finding the path with reasons to win, in retrospect, optimized my luck for the upside.

On the scholarship side, I graduated with the highest academic performance in my high school, spent thousands of hours volunteering as a musician, and led a community with more than a hundred cadets. On the bursary side, my family income was exceptionally low, which was a criterion for many bursaries. Had I not had such unfair advantages, taking other paths like working on farms or teaching aviation could have been better options to realize my upside. Prioritize opportunities where you have unfair advantages—find reasons to win.

Reason to Invest: Building Conviction Through Idea Mazes

Rejecting definitionally non-asymmetric opportunities and picking the winners are usually enough to arrive on a good starting point for experiments. But for larger, more complex swings, it's worth iterating scenario forecast to create a mental model to build enough conviction to start investing in your path. The examples I've shared so far have a single iteration of forecasts: upside, base, and downside. But now imagine each of those forecasts having a second set of forecasts. Recall my example of writing from Chapters 3 and 4, where each scenario led to an additional set of new scenarios. But instead of reactively adjusting to new opportunities, it's forecasting them from the very beginning. The theory of start-ups calls this the idea maze.

The idea maze is often attributed to Balaji Srinivasan, the former CTO of Coinbase and general partner at Andreessen Horowitz. In his view, outsiders only see a solid, realized path through the maze taken by the company. Outsiders rarely think about the other paths that could have occurred. They only make assessments based on the realized outcome, rather than the outcome compared to all that could happen. Kind of how you'd only see my realized path with my start-up and my book from Chapter 3, had I not shared the possible scenarios that were going through my mind. An idea maze is about becoming an insider to that process and seeing all the ways in which you can take your life or company. Here's how Balaji describes the idea maze:

"A bird's eye view of the idea maze, understanding all the permutations of the idea and the branching of the decision tree, gaming things out to the end of each scenario. Anyone can point out the entrance to the maze, but few can think through all the branches."[5]

If scenario forecasting was sampling for a single iteration of possible outcomes for a given opportunity, the idea maze is sampling scenario's scenario—a derivative of sorts. When you do, you'll have a sense of the range of scenarios that'll play out over longer periods of time, and adjust accordingly with new information. Before starting my start-up, I ran a similar exercise. It was a fintech that provided credit and funding to non-salaried employees, like creators. I had Letter of Intents in place for financing figured out with debt facilities and a pilot with a management company; credit models to assess risk and legal financial structures to send and retrieve cash; and the interface and product scopes for the experiment.

But for a more familiar illustration of the idea maze, I'll take a less technical and more intuitive example. Let's suppose you want to start writing online with a goal of earning $10,000 a month. Everyone starts with the same goal, but the idea maze would place you far ahead in the game, with multiple iterations or "nodes" of scenario forecasts. Each of these decisions should consider trade-offs that bring you closer to your goal in theory. A simple visualized version could look like Figure 6.1.

Let's say your first node is choosing between long- and shortform writing, each with their trade-offs. Let's say you chose longform writing. The next node may be choosing between formats, say essays, blogging, or newsletters. The node after that may be choosing platforms like Medium or Substack. Let's say you choose essays on Medium. Then you list a few dozen topics you could write about, and say you chose tech. And so on and so on. This simple illustration covers just one path of several hundred permutations. We haven't even gotten to monetization or marketing yet.

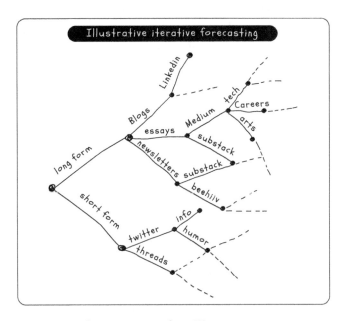

Figure 6.1   Iterative Forecasting Tree

In this example, each node should consider the perceived trade-offs for the best path to achieve the $10,000 monthly goal, with precise hypotheses on why one path would be better than another. As an extension, if one of your hypotheses (or understanding of trade-offs) happens to be wrong, then your idea maze can easily calculate the impacts, and make adjustments accordingly. Let's push the example a bit further. Suppose you chose Medium as your primary platform, because you believe your essay style writing is best suited to generate revenue through their payout program. Let's say you put this to the test. In reality, let's say people read the bullet-point summary you've placed in the beginning, and rarely read beyond that. You'd learn that your audience likes to read short, bullet-point summaries, and not blocks of text. You'll also learn that your monetization will be punished by Medium for short read times. Suppose then, dozens of brands start reaching out for placement—which Medium frowns upon—in the summary section of your essay. You'd probably want to scrap the essay and focus on the summary everyone finds valuable and choose a platform that freely allows brand sponsorships. Outcomes of your experiment should give you direction on where to go next. An idea maze helps you pinpoint exactly which assumptions were wrong, and how to backtrack based on the new information because you've run through all the trade-offs at every node. When you run a detailed single-path hypothesis, a single "wrong" hypothesis can derail your entire path. In contrast, the idea maze is like having an entire map with a GPS. You know exactly where you are in the maze of possible outcomes, and avoid starting from scratch every time you're proven wrong.

That said, the idea maze isn't the right tool for everything, especially if it comes at the price of large delays to running experiments. Between the two extremes of fast experiments with no thought vs. slow experiments with too much thought lies an optimal point in the spectrum. That's where good experiments live. Though, I think for larger swings, having an idea maze in place will allow you to be faster in the long run because you will have a full understanding of the problem space. That's a great starting point to start experimenting— when everything works, at least in theory.

Good Experiment = Viable and Iterative

The collection of your hypotheses, if correct, should bound future outcomes within the range of your scenario forecasts. And if you manage to prove out every assumption of your Need-to-Believe analysis in your favor, then you should necessarily realize your upside. Experiments are about testing these hypotheses that already work in theory. Each experiment should strengthen or adjust your understanding of the world.

Good Experiments

Every once in a while, I come across people who say, "I'm just running an experiment." My usual follow-up is, "What's your thesis on what will happen?" to which I'm met with "I don't know, we'll find out."

That's great.

Except that it's missing the defining characteristic of an experiment: to corroborate or disprove a hypothesis. Not all experiments are equal. There is such a thing as good and bad experiments. The marks of a good experiment in the context of Asymmetric Principles come with a delicate balance between *conviction* and *efficiency* of experiments.

Good Experiments Lead to Conviction Remember from Chapter 5 that you want to avoid both Type I and Type II errors: You don't want to pursue a dead-end path, but you also don't want to reject a path that could take you to your upside. Good experiments provide confidence to either continue down the current path or change directions of a particular path in your idea maze. Poor experiments add little confidence in either direction.

Consequently, good experiments tend to be tightly scoped, testing one or two hypotheses at a time for convictions. For example, suppose I wanted to run experiments on a series of hypotheses that would lead to the success of my book. Using a single experiment to test several hypotheses, like—will a (1) specific audience (2) value the content I write (3) in the format of a book (4) in a particular sales channel—would dilute the information.

With so many variables at play, interpreting the outcome to build conviction one way or another would be challenging. Was it because of the right audience or despite the wrong audience? Was it because of the right sales channel or despite the wrong ones? And so on. Conviction on a single hypothesis is better than mixed signals across many hypotheses. But, if the goal is maximizing conviction, why not design experiments that give you a near 100% conviction on a single variable? That's because of efficiency.

Good Experiments are Efficient   In Chapter 5, I introduced systems venture capitalists use to optimize their resources: progressively increasing the amount of time on a company only if they continue to validate their investment thesis (collection of hypotheses). Similarly, good experiments consider real-life constraints on resources, designed for enough conviction for the next level of investment. It's akin to the trade-off of sampling a population and extrapolating the truth than testing with the whole 8 billion.

Suppose I wanted to run an experiment to test if readers would value the content of my writing. Well, if I want to maximize conviction and refuse to rely on proxies, the experiment would probably entail writing the entire book to run the experiment. That would be awfully inefficient, and even then, it would test one of many hypotheses that need to be true. Efficient experiments are sampled, imperfect proxies to test reality to manage limited resources. Of course, the threshold should be high enough to give *some* direction to invest more time into it. For example, a fast, low-cost experiment of asking my friends "would you buy my book" without any details about the book wouldn't provide conviction in either direction, even if the answer was "yes, absolutely."

Another element of efficiency is minimizing the number of experiments for an answer. If there are 100 hypotheses, you probably don't need to run all 100 before building conviction to double down or move on. The order of operations in which hypotheses to test first matter here. Be biased toward hypotheses that can give you early direction with minimal effort and before testing the ones with the highest sensitivity for the rest of your decision tree. By sensitivity, I'm borrowing the concept from financial modeling: how a single percentage change in an input variable impacts the outcome. This sounds obvious, but there is temptation to avoid the most important questions, because it might point to an undesirable answer. Don't ignore the elephant in the room.

Good experiments balance both conviction and efficiency. Taking the good starting points and running good experiments is exactly how early-stage founders find their initial traction. They run minimum, viable, and iterative experiments.

The Minimum Viable Experiment

The Minimum Viable Product or MVP is a framework start-up founders use to design experiments: balancing capital and speed with level of confidence in accepting or rejecting a hypothesis. The *minimum* is there to optimize for speed of testing to maximize iterations under constraints, and *viable* is there to ensure the iteration of experiment provides conviction. The purpose is to prevent founders from making Type I and Type II errors: prematurely walking away from a billion-dollar idea and getting stuck for too long and foregoing billion-dollar ideas.

The founders of DoorDash, a food delivery app and SoftBank portfolio company, killed it with their early experiments. Testing the first of their many hypotheses, the founders were validating if delivery in their local area, Palo Alto, would solve an actually painful problem. The threshold was: "will people pay for it?" Instead of building a full app and logistics systems for maximal conviction, founders created a scrappy version by putting up a website called PaloAltoDelivery.com with menus from local restaurants and a number to call in an order. The founders would take the order, call the restaurant, pick up the order, and deliver it to the customer with a flat charge for the deliveries.[6] The test was *minimal* in putting as little work building something as possible and *viable* with a binary test of "is food delivery valuable enough for people to pay?" With convictions from early experiments, the founders continued their journey, until it has become a $50 billion company in 2024.[7]

Like DoorDash, experimental design in your life will be more of an art than a science. Start with the most material hypotheses in your idea maze, and run a narrow, minimal experiment, where the outcomes would provide you with just enough conviction and information to point you in the right direction despite incomplete data and scarce resources. With these general principles in mind, let's dive deeper into how viability and minimum characteristics integrate into actual life decisions.

Viability: Getting Good Reps

Without viability, it doesn't matter how many "experiments" you run. The viability of an experiment means the outcomes give you enough confidence to pursue or abandon your path. The immediate practical concerns are picking the right metric, which should be trackable and approximate reality; and picking the right threshold, which balances enough conviction to invest more, with resources to get to that conviction. I'll take what's salient on my mind as I write this chapter.

Can I Become a Best–Selling Author?　　Book sales will be top of mind for me over the next few quarters, leading up to and after the publication of this book. My editor tells me that 10,000 copies is the magic number. A rudimentary *Need-to-Believe* might look like a funnel. I'd reach a certain number of people, of which a certain percentage convert to purchasing a book, until I hit the target number of 10,000 books. Of course, there is considerable detail (from the types of audiences to an array of sales channels I should consider) but it comes down to a function of *total reach* and *conversion rates*. For example, a 10% conversion rate would imply I need to reach 100,000 people, while a 1% conversion implies reaching a million people to hit the target 10,000 books. So that's a sensitive variable.

Let's suppose my hypothesis is reaching a blended 2% reach-to-sales conversion rate across different sales channels. A poor experiment would be going up to 10 of my closest friends and asking "Hey I'm writing a book. Would you buy it?" with 100% of them saying "Yes." Accepting this proxy, and adjusting my hypothesis from a 2% conversion rate to a 100% conversion rate, and adjusting the target reach to 10,000 people would be a mistake. Instead, metrics should reflect reality and be grounded in quantitative metrics.

A better way to run an experiment is to replicate the mechanics of a "reach-to-sale," which requires someone to act, often in a way that costs them something. That could be as simple as sending a sign-up link to 1,000 people to receive an email for when my book launches. Now I have data. Did people click the link? Did they sign up? If the conversion rate for spending 30 seconds to sign up is 2%, the conversion rate of purchasing the book with far more clicks and dollars would be far lower than 2%. I could run similar experiments for other channels from targeted ads to newsletters to book clubs to test that conversion. Based on the outcomes of those experiments, I'd adjust my *Need-to-Believe* analysis and strategies accordingly. For example, perhaps the two best channels from my experiments convert at 1.25% and all other channels didn't even reach 0.1%. I'd abandon all other channels to focus on these two channels. I'd then adjust my target reach from at least 500,000 people (2% conversion rate) to 800,000. Of course, the information is imperfect, and it's open to change at scale, but it would give enough direction to move forward. In this example, I've stressed using quantifiable metrics to ground oneself in objectivity. But sometimes, reliance on subjectivity is required, and should come with understanding of their risks.

The Coffee Detective   Choosing the right metrics without verifiable data is hard because people lie, intentionally or not. Studies show people lie several times a day. Even if people want to tell the truth, people are bad at answering hypotheticals. If I were to ask a room, "Would you have owned slaves as a Greek or Roman citizen during the Greco-Roman world?" the total number of yeses would be far lower than the estimates of 25% of the population[8] who did own slaves during that time. We need not look so far back in history. There are far more people who would claim they would be Schindler than the number of Schindlers that are historically accounted for. Amid tragedies during 2024, we're observing the real-time disparity between proclaimed virtues and realized virtues. These are extreme examples, but people tend to lie for a variety of reasons. That includes when you test hypotheses by talking to people. Rob Fitzpatrick, in his book *The Mom Test*, addresses precisely this problem, and the book has become a bible for start-up founders to ask good questions and design good experiments that align with reality.[9] I'll share my own hypothetical example, perhaps of a coffee detective.

Imagine you're on your way to work on a Monday morning, and you see everyone is holding a cup of coffee—including you. Why is coffee $8? Everyone you know complains about the price. Even finance gurus keep telling you to stop buying coffee. Do you have a billion-dollar idea on your hands?

Let's say one of your many hypotheses to build a coffee empire is that people would choose your coffee if it was cheaper. Rather than asking people, "Would you buy my coffee if it's the same quality for 50% cheaper" and counting the number of "Yeses" as your metric, a better experiment would be establishing facts—like a detective trying to find the truth. Questions like "How many cups of coffee did you drink yesterday? This week?" "Where do you get your coffee?" "What time of day do you find yourself drinking coffee?" "Why did you choose the coffee you're drinking now?" will bring you closer to the approximation of the truth and give you insight on your hypothesis.

So it could be that some people would answer "yes" to your initial survey of "Would you buy coffee that is 50% cheaper with better quality?" But reality, based on factual questions, will be much more nuanced. For example, a person might respond "yes" even if they:

- Don't actually drink coffee, but think coffee is generally overpriced.
- Drink coffee every weekday morning, but only in the office because it's provided for free, and caffeine helps them concentrate.
- Only buy coffee from this one shop because they use a rare type of beans and would prefer it if it were cheaper.
- Made friends with the barista at a local coffee shop, and exclusively buys coffee from there, but cheaper coffee would be nicer.
- Purchase coffee because it's on their route to a workout, and loyalty points are nice for an occasional free coffee.

As you can see, questions that aren't grounded in facts, open too much room for lies and bad approximations of hypotheticals. What you actually want to test is "Will enough people buy *my* coffee if it's cheaper?" Asking the right questions grounded in facts can actually answer that question.

Another way to cut through the lies is to emulate the purchase by getting people to commit to what they say. If someone says they love your idea and would absolutely buy your coffee, *The Mom Test* would advise that you push for a commitment like buying your coffee today for the discounted price, or pre-ordering your coffee that will be released in three months, or commit them to a monthly subscription plan to have it delivered, or at the very least to promote the coffee on their social media. It mimics the actual purchase process, and creates skin in the game by investing their dollars, reputation, or something else of value for conviction that your hypothesis is correct. The coffee example is biased toward experiments designed to provide a service or product. But its principles of viability can be applied to most experiments from choosing a career path to starting a side gig to moving cities.

For your experiments to count, they need to be viable. Metrics should be grounded in truth with the closest approximation to reality, that balance conviction and efficiency for a path forward. Once you have viability, the minimum becomes important to maximize your probabilities of quickly finding the right hypotheses.

The Minimum: Iterative Cycles

Viability isn't license to spend an eternity designing the perfect experiment. If you have a hundred hypotheses, and it takes you a year to get through one, you'll run out of years before you can prove anything. The winning strategy (of the right balance of perfection and speed) is based on the type of game we're playing.

In game theory, a strategy is described as *dominant* or *dominated* in relation to available choices. For example, a weakly dominant strategy gives an equal or better outcome than a weakly dominated strategy: heads I win big, tails I still win small. The same strategy can be dominant or dominated depending on the type of game being played. The optimal strategy will be different depending on the game. One way to categorize games is by its iteration: single, finitely iteratively, or infinitely iterative.

Most games in life are finitely iterative, meaning a set of repeated games that have an end. For these games, taking multiple shots weakly dominates a perfect single shot. The theory of start-ups, like many life decisions, assumes a finitely iterative game. That's where the adage of "fail fast"—learn that your hypotheses were wrong sooner than later—comes from in the start-up world. To do that, experiments need to be minimal to optimize for speed. By launching as many minimal, but viable experiments as possible, you can arrive at the truth faster. Considerable case studies of start-up success from such minimally viable experiments exist—to the point it's a core part of the theory of start-ups. In fact, it scales to massive technology companies as well. One example is A/B testing, which is a mass iteration experiment across groups of users (A and B) to test what changes optimize the usage of their platform right down to the color of the buttons. Iterative experimentation isn't a dominant strategy unique to the start-up world, with a much wider conceptual applicability.

Elmo's Scheme   After indulging in a wildly overpriced cheese fondue by the banks of Limmat, I wandered into the Kunsthaus Art Museum to walk off the calories. My eyes widened at the sight of a Sesame Street exhibition. Pictures of Elmo stirred up childhood memories. I first learned English through the familiar voices of the show. Little did I know that Sesame Street was meticulously designed by researchers to make it one of the most successful, longest-running educational TV shows in the world.

"The Distractor" by James Bridle is an installation in the Kunsthaus that documents *formative evaluation*, which incorporates highly iterative ways to create content, considered a novel application in educational television in the 1960s.[10] Led by Edward L. Palmer, a Harvard professor, researchers screened segments of an episode to daycares and schools with slide shows of random images, which were called distractors. Researchers then observed which screens children focused on to assess engagement; they then gave short tests before and after the segment to measure educational impact. Producers then iterated until an episode scored more than 90% attention score over the distractor before releasing it to the general public. Highly iterative approaches made *Sesame Street* one of the most successful educational TV shows that made a difference in many lives of children—including in mine.[11] Iterating viable experiments is such a powerful approach, in fact, it enables kindergarteners to crush post-graduate professionals.

Spaghetti and Tape   Tom Wujec, a fellow Manitoban, popularized a design experiment called the Marshmallow Challenge,[12] originally created by Peter Skillman, who led design at the executive level at several prominent organizations like Microsoft, Amazon, IDEO, Nokia, and currently at Philips. The experiment was to see which groups perform better in building a tower that can withhold the weight of a single marshmallow, all within 18 minutes with the following:

- 20 sticks of spaghetti
- 90 cm in tape
- 90 cm of string

Groups of MBAs, kindergarteners, architects and engineers, and executives took on the experience (Figure 6.2.). Guess how they all did?

The kindergartners built towers much taller than the average of groups of lawyers and MBAs.[13] What drove the success? The heights of the towers were positively correlated to the number of iterations trying to build the tower. The groups with more cycles of iterating on

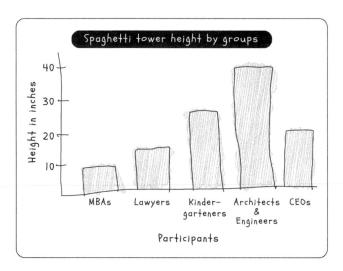

Figure 6.2   Spaghetti Tower Height by Groups

a prototype built taller towers in the 18-minute time allotment. Once you've hit the minimum viability, take the shot and improve as quickly as you can.

Order of Operations   If my hand was forced to choose between viability and minimum characteristics, I'd say viability comes before iterations. In a variation of the Marshmallow Experiment, designers introduced a $10,000 prize for winners to increase the pressure, which led to poor performance—not short towers, but no towers at all, leaving no tower to improve on.[14] Viability for conviction comes first before the minimum, because without viability, the number of iterations and cost don't really matter. When the first tower was not viable, iterative improvement from a nonviable tower doesn't work. The pressure to move quickly can sometimes lead to poor experiments. Set viability first, and maximize iteration with minimal design.

Minimum viable experiments seem to work in start-ups, in television, and apparently in spaghetti towers. How does that apply in running good experiments in the context of *Asymmetric Principles* in life decisions? The goal is getting to a reliable answer quickly that points you in the right direction.

Dodging a Career Bullet

Before starting college, I liked the idea of being a lawyer. I cold emailed a few dozen attorneys for advice and their experience working as a lawyer. That was an early experiment, and I kept law school as an option. By my senior year of college, I had to make a decision, with both Type I and II errors at hand on pursuing law:

- **Type I:** Spend weeks studying for the LSAT and applying to law schools only to find out I hated the law.
- **Type II:** Miss out on a career that could be fulfilling to me.

The threshold to pursue law was high because I already knew I liked strategy consulting based on my internship at The Boston Consulting Group. Before writing off becoming a lawyer completely, I invested time to speak with law students and lawyers in my school. That changed the trade-offs of my decision node in my idea maze dramatically. It turns out that the UK doesn't require a three-year law degree before you can start practicing law. Instead, a one-year Graduate Diploma in Law (GDL) was enough to start a paid traineeship at a law firm. Better yet, large corporate law firms in the UK, known as the Magic Circle, would sponsor my education. So instead of sinking three years in law school with hundreds of thousands of dollars, I could have a law firm pay for my legal education and try corporate law within 12 months. With an offer from a consulting firm in hand, I submitted a few applications to law firms in the UK.

In early January, Clifford Chance, one of the Magic Circle law firms, flew me out to London for an *Assessment Day* interview. After a red eye from Montreal to Gatwick, I took the train to a rundown hotel with windowless rooms—and it definitely did not have early check-in policies. I freshened up in the stall-less lobby bathroom, awkwardly locking eyes with confused strangers as I changed into my suit. But these petty nuisances didn't dampen my unfledged excitement of seeing London for the first time—not even the underwhelming English breakfast. Satisfied with my first corporate-reimbursed breakfast, I walked over to 10 Upper Bank Street, one of many high-rises in Canary Wharf.

By noon, Oxbridge students surrounded me, intrigued by the only foreigner with a telling Canadian accent. From then, I started a full day of interviews with a half-dozen attorneys at the firm, and focused on my objective. As an interviewee, I used my license to ask questions in full, to fill the gaps of my *Need-to-Believe* analysis—the daily tasks, nature of the work, progression, compensation, and so on—to determine whether to take the role. By the end of the day, I had enough information to conclude that I'd enjoy consulting more than law, at least when it came to the nature of the work for junior associates.

To be clear, I didn't receive the offer. But that's okay, because rather than spending months setting up calls with partner-level attorneys who charge thousands of dollars an hour or spending years in law school, I came to a conclusion within a day by running a minimum, viable experiment—oh, and a free trip to London. Real life has unknown unknowns, and is often hairier than you think, especially when you apply it in your own life with specific circumstances. *Asymmetric Principles* provides the framework to navigate and find your early sets of upsides. But I recognize my example may seem too specific. For a less precise, but more generalized illustration, I'll share a high-level hypothetical of riding a strong tailwind. Boom cycles will pop up, with AI being the most prevalent one today in 2024. Minimal, iterative experiments will give you conviction to ride or pass on these tailwinds.

During the recent tech boom in 2019, everyone wanted to move into tech. The flexible work environment and extravagant perks coupled with high salaries and prestige made it an attractive place to be. Suppose you wanted to take a swing and see if you could build the skills to join one of these companies. An example of a *nonviable* experiment is browsing Reddit for a day and ruling out that you're not interested, or you wouldn't make it. An example of a *nonminimal* experiment is completing a four-year computer science degree to assess if you like it, and to join a tech company. While I'm not claiming this is THE right experiment, a better alternative than either experiment could have been bootcamps, which run over a few months with the goal of placing students in a tech company. Often these were structured in a way that charged nothing upfront, and provided a payment plan as an income-share-agreement *after* the program—but only if you end up landing a job above a reasonable salary threshold in the tech industry.

At the end of the day, experiments are all about execution. Many intelligent people have been trapped by hypotheses without testing them against the real world. There are many ways to run experiments.

In fact, some people brute force this entire process by moving at a velocity orders of magnitude faster than others. However, the framework of minimally viable experiments in the context of *Asymmetric Principles* is one that has been tested to consistently and reliably maximize your chances of finding right paths in your idea maze. It's designed to balance convictions in your path with efficiency of resources to arrive at your very first upsides as you apply *Asymmetric Principles* in life.

Concluding Hypotheses and Experiments

Theory of start-ups is a collection of highly tested hypotheses that enable start-ups to consistently realize their initial traction despite the odds. Taking the pertinent aspects as the foundational model, I've created the framework for applying *Asymmetric Principles* to structurally place you in the path of luck to realize your very first upsides. Good hypotheses and good experiments are systems I've personally used to build my start-up and to make major life decisions. I have conviction that people who consistently build good hypotheses and execute good experiments will have a high likelihood of consistently finding early upsides in their lives.

In opening this chapter, I contended that every system has trade-offs, each with its limitations. The system of good hypotheses and good experiments is optimized to find your very first set of upsides or what theory of start-ups might call *initial traction*. However, it's an appallingly inefficient one to scale that initial traction into Super Upsides. In fact, in realms of start-ups, Paul Graham describes the traction finding process in a famous essay titled *Do Things That Don't Scale*,[15] quite literally pointing out that these systems of iterative experiments are not designed to scale. Chapter 6 was about systems optimized for your first upsides. In the next chapter, I will discuss systems of leverage to sustainably scale your upsides all the way to the Super Upside—from the local to global maxima.

7 | Scaling with Momentum and Leverage

"Give me a lever long enough and a place to stand, and I will move the earth"

—Archimedes

Creating Momentum

When enough of your early hypotheses have been wrong, corrected, and validated, the idea maze in your head aligns closely enough with reality—that's when things click. Founders call these flickers, *traction*. It's comparable to the excitement you'd feel seeing smoke after hours of rubbing two sticks together. Once you have traction, the key is growing the fragile ember into flames. Paul Graham, in his essay, describes this process with a metaphor: "A good metaphor would be the cranks that car engines had before they got electric starters. Once the engine was going, it would keep going, but there was a separate and laborious process to get it going."

The amount of energy required to create early traction can be analogous to creating momentum with escape velocity of a spaceship. Don't let it flame out. Once you've created traction, maintaining momentum is one of the most important things you can do for at least two reasons: it ignites passion and creates inertia.

Momentum Ignites Passion

Passion is a word that gets thrown around, especially in contexts of leadership and career development. There seems to be this myth that finding a life-long passion is step one to doing anything great. And maybe that's why every grad school application and job cover letter is riddled with "ever since I can remember" and "since I was a child," which seem to perpetuate this myth of a defined, specific passion, on which one can bet one's life.

While I concede that this is certainly a possibility for some, my position is that passion often comes in broad strokes of innate interests, which are developed into specific passions from experiences, learnings, and rewards. It seems doubtful that every science student had a rather specific passion to become a plastic surgeon that happens to earn seven figures. That's not to say rewards are vain, but that they should be properly acknowledged in their role in building passion. In fact, one of the best rewards, especially relevant to *Asymmetric Principles*, comes from rapid growth. When you start growing quickly, it becomes fun. And when it becomes fun, you become "passionate" about it. I don't think B2B SaaS founders had a genetic predisposition to be passionate about esoteric accounting or HR payroll. But when you start doubling your growth every few months, with a clear path toward becoming a billion-dollar company, I imagine you learn to be passionate about what you're doing. Passion follows momentum.

What Stays in Motion Remains in Motion

The second benefit of creating and maintaining momentum is inertia generated from momentum. Inertia allows you to scale much faster with much less effort. It's a lot easier to grow the fire than starting one. When I started writing on Medium, finding my first 100 followers to start monetizing took the most amount of effort. Even after monetization, making the hundred dollars was harder than the next thousand for Medium. Reward to work ratio improves dramatically with momentum.

By the very nature of rapid growth, rewards tend to be concentrated toward the end. For instance, my seed round for my start-up was oversubscribed with more than $5 million in written commitments in a little more than a week. But I didn't close capital commitments at a linear rate of $500,000 a day until then. Almost the entire commitment ballooned in the last few days.

As you can see, the growth rates of asymmetric opportunities are rarely linear, but rather flat until it becomes exponential after an inflection point. A close comparison is pushing a piece of rock uphill until it tips over the other side. Not only do you no longer push, but you'll see speed accelerate once you hit that tipping point. Start-ups call that *product market fit*. Momentum will push for you. That's why going full throttle to keep momentum is important.

Don't Lose Momentum

On the flipside of that, losing momentum is demoralizing. Picture the crushing despair you'd feel, watching the last wisp of smoke fleeing from your lifeless embers, with full knowledge of the work it'll take to rekindle that first spark.

An equivalent life decision is losing focus. The worst thing you can do is be distracted from your first set of upsides. There will always be the next shiny thing, and people come to you with new sticks to rub together. But don't make the mistake of neglecting the very reason they want to be with you in the first place—the spark. If you lose momentum, it can be exceptionally hard to get it back. Don't take your foot off the gas.

From Local to Global Maxima

Momentum, along with the rapidly growing nature of *Asymmetric Principles*, will push your growth until the natural limit of your existing systems. That's your local maxima—the *structural limit* of the system that constrains your potential. For example, if your work involves your time, you'll hit a physical limit at the 24-hour daily limit—and in practice, much earlier, if you incorporate necessities of food, sleep, and exercise. You cannot increase that 24-hour daily limit. The limitation is structural.

In the case of my writing, I hit that limit quite quickly. My priority was working on my start-up, so allocating only a few hours a month on writing didn't take long to approach that limit. But even if I had decided to stop everything and invest all my time in writing, reaching structural limits would only be a matter of time. The systems to find your traction from Chapter 6 of good hypotheses and good experiments have local maxima far below your Super Upside. That's a feature, not a bug. Recall that every system has trade-offs. The initial system was optimized to find initial traction through high iteration of minimum viable experiments, rather than effectively scaling. That's for good reason.

Given the high "expected failure rate" of *Asymmetric Principles*, it is inefficient to build scalable systems for every experiment. You'd want a scrappy, minimum viable version, to iterate as quickly as it can. Imagine spending a few hours manually to iterate on the design, color, and material of an espresso cup to experiment with the one that'll be most popular. Handcrafting cups isn't scalable, but it'll help you find your first product faster than spending six months negotiating a deal with a factory to produce 100,000 units every time you make a design change. As we discussed in Chapter 6, it would make sense to iterate manually until finding an espresso cup people like—your initial traction—even if it isn't scalable.

But when things start to scale with momentum, switching the system optimized for rapid experimentation to the system designed to scale is necessary to go beyond local maxima to global maxima. The alternative is being bound by structural limits, and eventually losing momentum. Imagine trying to handcraft 100,000 espresso cups a year by yourself. You'd not only hit your structural limit—physically impossible—but also burn out pretty quickly if you tried to scale this way. Adam Grant, in his book *Hidden Potential,* describes a similar phenomenon in the context of growing a skillset:

"Skills don't grow at a steady pace. Improving them is like driving up a mountain. As we climb higher and higher, the road gets steeper and steeper, and our gains get smaller and smaller. When we run out of momentum, we start to stall. It's not enough to step on the gas—our wheels are spinning, but we've stopped moving."[1]

Breaking out of your local maxima may seem like an obvious point, but it's hard in practice. You've probably mastered the system that got you there, and you'll need to slow down in your busiest time to adopt new systems, especially as you near the upper limits of your current system. But you'll need to change systems to hit your global maxima.

Slow Down to Go Higher, Farther, Safer

When I was 17, I was one of the few lucky Royal Canadian Air Cadets to be funded by the Canadian Department of National Defence to become a pilot. Its history traces back to World War II to train young pilots to join the Royal Canadian Air Force.[2] While today, it's no longer a part of the military, one in five private pilots in Canada and 67% of commercial pilots in Canada are graduates of this program.[3]

In my early days of training as a pilot, the primary method of navigation was through Visual Flight Rules or VFR. VFR simply means looking out the cockpit window for visual cues to identify my position—the altitude, attitude, and pitch of the aircraft—relative to my surroundings. Under VFR, my navigation is driven by visual cues, making corrections as needed, running on "That mountain must be the one I see on this map. Let's not run into that" or "Oh, there's the lake, so that's the one. I'll need to course correct by a few degrees east." This is a fast and intuitive way to navigate, and works quite well until about, say, 10,000 feet, but it certainly will not work at 30,000 feet on both practical and legal grounds. And VFR comes with several other restrictions and limitations as well, like being unable to navigate in the clouds or after sunset. Flying beyond those structural limits can be disastrous—like a graveyard spiral, where a disoriented pilot unknowingly spirals the plane toward the ground after losing all visual references in the clouds. Or worse, harming my passengers or jeopardizing other aircraft.

To fly higher, farther, and safer, pilots adopt a new system called Instrument Flight Rules or IFR, which relies on instruments to understand position relative to surroundings. It gives pilots flexibility to enter Class A airspaces, usually above 18,000 feet, and allows greater flexibility even when visual reference points are unavailable.

The problem is that transitioning from VFR to IFR impacts flight performance before ramping up again. Not only that, but every pilot will also tell you how boring IFR can be, relying on radio and instruments rather than enjoying the view. I dreaded IFR training that required putting on funky glasses that blocked out the cockpit view.

It will be tempting to stick with the system you've mastered and the system that got you where you are. But reaching the natural limit of your system means stepping on the gas alone isn't enough. You need to change systems. As the Navy SEAL's mantra suggests: "slow is smooth and smooth is fast."[4] Don't cap your Super Upside because you're afraid to slow down. Adoption of systems to scale is necessary if you want to go higher, farther, safer.

Scaling with Leverage

Leverage is perhaps one of the best systems designed to scale beyond structural limits of most systems. It's a concept that has been beaten to death, yet still manages to be misunderstood, probably because of its imprecise language, and ubiquitous use. I'll kick off this section to be as precise with different types of leverage and walk through how to appropriately apply it to scale your upside.

Etymologically, leverage is used to describe mechanical advantage in using a lever to raise objects in the realms of physics. But the vernacular use in media usually refers to leverage applied in the world of finance to generate greater return than traditionally possible. Let's take two investment opportunities to compare leveraged and non-leveraged investments. In the non-leveraged case, imagine an opportunity to invest $5. If things go well, you can double it. If things go poorly, you'll lose your $5. So if you win, your return is 2×. Now imagine a leveraged case, where you take $1 and borrow the remaining $4 to invest in the same opportunity as the first case. So, if you win, you'll get $10. After returning the $4 you borrowed, you end up with a 6× return on your dollar instead of 2× in the unleveraged case. That's the simplest form of what private equity firms do all day through Leverage Buyout or LBO (with considerably more complexity).

For *Asymmetric Principles*, leverage is a horrible system to start with, because leverage generated *symmetrical* outsized outcomes. It doesn't discriminate against generating outsized upsides or downsides. To revisit the example above, imagine the investment going to zero. Instead of having a net 0% in an unleveraged case, you'll be left with −400% in debt in a leveraged one. There is a reason why I waited to introduce leverage until now, after you find your initial set of upsides. Order of operations matter.

In the context of *Asymmetric Principles* where the expectation is that most of your experiments will fail, using leverage almost always leads to overall bad outcomes. That's the importance of precision. Use leverage when you are scaling, not experimenting.

Leverage in Life Decisions

Leverage allows you to increase the size of outcomes, while holding your input steady in your life. My priority is my start-up, which left little room for anything else. Leverage is how I managed to write a book despite a structural limit placed by six hours a month or 15 minutes a day. Publishing a book takes considerable amount of work, and on my own would have taken several years. That was my base case, writing bits and pieces on Medium with relevant scenario forecasts from Chapter 3. But significant *leverage* from a large publisher allowed me to publish a book, a rather large outcome, from the 15-minutes-a-day commitment:

- A team of designers worked on the cover design and the figures
- A development editor gave me feedback chapter by chapter
- A copy editor reviewed grammar and consistency ("startup vs. start-up"), and tidied up the end notes
- A production team will index and work with the printing presses
- A managing editor registered my book on all major bookstores with a schedule to be shipped on the launch date
- A publicist is pitching my book for awards and lists

As a first-time author, I also benefit from the reputation of the publisher. Iteratively experimenting with writing on 15 minutes a day had capped upsides. But using leverage with my initial traction enabled me to generate a far outsized return. Because of that, I could focus my attention on writing and promoting my book, rather than diverting my attention elsewhere, like working out placements in physical bookstores or calling up printing presses. Now, to be clear, leverage comes at a cost. I had to give up a large portion of my royalties to benefit from leverage. But this sort of leverage is what allowed me to publish a book on 15 minutes a day while running my start-up.

Even in this example, the precise mechanisms of leverage are muddled because there are several forms of leverage at play. Observed impact of leverage in life often has a *blended* impact from different types of leverage, making the distinct impacts harder to observe. In the next section, I'll isolate the types of leverage and the characteristics of each to effectively apply leverage for the *scaling stage* of *Asymmetric Principles*.

Types of Leverage

Many thinkers, including Naval Ravikant, contextualized the use of leverage to scale outcomes for individual lives and careers. Naval is the founder of AngelList, a multibillion-dollar company that connects start-up fundraising with angel investors.[5] While I generally agree with his high-level thoughts on leverage, I've expanded on the framework, detailing and adding to the types of leverage and their trade-offs, which I've summarized in Table 7.1, that will serve as the focal point of this section.

Table 7.1   Types of Leverage

Types of Leverage	Scaling Trajectory	Characteristics
• Labor	• Scales linearly due to high marginal costs of time as base unit	• Rivalrous, permissioned, non-fungible
• Capital	• Scales geometrically due to low marginal costs of capital as base unit	• Semi-rivalrous, permissioned, fungible
• Software and Content	• Scales exponentially due to near-zero marginal cost of code and media as base unit	• Non-rivalrous, permissionless, fungible

For clarity on terminology in Table 7.1, each characteristic is in context of the base unit of each leverage type.

- "Rivalrous" refers to the economic definition, which is a resource that can only be consumed by one person or entity at a time. That means use of that resource reduces its availability for use by others. For example, if I spend an hour working with you, I cannot use that same hour working with someone else. I'd be left with 23 hours for that day.
- "Permissioned" refers to access to the resource, and an aspect Naval emphasizes. The provider of leverage must give the user permission to borrow or use the resource. For example, employees give permission to employers to use labor and time under an employment contract.
- "Fungible" refers to how flexible the base unit can be converted into other forms of leverage or resources.
- "Marginal cost" is an economic concept that refers to cost of generating an additional unit of a resource. For this context, cost to replicate is a close enough definition.

Definitions should become clearer as we explore the types of leverage.

Labor Leverage

Labor has a base unit of time. Labor leverage is simply borrowing other people's time or expertise. It can be as simple as hiring a cleaning professional or as complex as outsourcing entire company divisions. Because the base unit of it is time, labor comes with a certain set of characteristics:

- **Labor is rivalrous:** If you use an hour of your time on work, you can't use that same hour to play. No one else can simultaneously use that time either.
- **Labor is permissioned:** You need to convince someone to give you permission to use their labor. Otherwise, it would be slavery.
- **Labor is not fungible:** Labor is hard to convert into any other forms of leverage. People rarely trade time for time.

Usually, labor leverage is used for substitution of time or expertise. The copyeditors who will review this book, for example, will provide a mix of both variations. The pure mechanical correction of grammar and spelling is closer to substitution of time (I could do it myself), while corrections related to industry standard end note styles and indexing would be in the realm of expertise. Another example of substitution and expertise distinction is hiring a babysitter compared to a lawyer. Presumably, you're just as good, and hopefully better, at parenting your own child than your babysitter. But perhaps you're substituting time so you can spend three hours with your significant other for a date night once a week. In contrast, hiring a law firm to solve a complex legal case is substituting expertise. Law firms have systems and processes that take far less time with far better outcomes than from your own labor.

Most people are, at least in part, labor providers, and provide leverage to others. That's not a bad thing. Anyone from factory workers, virtual assistants, bankers, and doctors provide a form of labor in exchange for some utility, typically a salary. It's the reason we don't have to be an expert in every aspect of our lives.

Labor Scales Linearly Because time is fixed and rivalrous, the marginal cost (cost of additional base unit of labor, in this time) of labor leverage tends to stay fixed, and even increase. At scale, it generally scales linearly.

Let's say you start tutoring students for $20 an hour (price), and you have a maximum of 40 hours a week to work (time). Once you hit your structural limit of 40 hours ($800 a week), the remaining lever to scale is price. Now, there are creative ways to effectively increase your average price per hour, like holding group sessions with multiple students instead of increasing your rate. For simplicity, let's say you raise the average price from $20 to $30 an hour with the weekly earnings of $1,200. That's more or less the limit of tutoring income from the current system.

If you want to scale with labor leverage, you can hire someone. Let's assume demand is not an issue, and you bring on a full-time tutor who will generate $1,200 a week. Let's say you split it evenly since you brought in the customers. You'd increase your earnings by $600 a week, bringing your total weekly income from $1,200 to $1,800. Every additional tutor scaling under these conditions will generate $1,200 of weekly income but cost you $600 a week. Even at scale, these marginal costs will remain the same, often leading to linear shaped growth in terms of dollars earned. But just because it scales linearly doesn't mean it can't grow to be massive.

Labor Leverage at Scale   Any professional service that charges for expertise and judgment relies on labor leverage. It would be strange to say McKinsey's $16 billion in 2023 revenue[6] to provide management consulting services or the Big Four accounting firms that collectively generated $200 billion of revenue[7] in 2023 didn't scale.

My first job out of college was at one of these consulting firms—a labor provider—Oliver Wyman. At the time, I came across my "daily rate," which is the price tag charged to the client for one day of my time. I calculated that my salary was less than 10% of that daily rate. What does that mean? Even with other costs like benefits and training, I was generating about a 90% gross margin for the company. The CEO of Oliver Wyman *could* draft every slide, close every sale, build every model, and run every interview, but it is far more valuable to hire consultants to do this at such margins. So, this is how labor leverage can scale at its best.

Trade-offs of Scaling with Labor Leverage   Labor leverage is simple, but scaling is hairy. It's not easy to convince people with high-caliber expertise to come work for you. Fundamentally, it's because labor leverage is what Naval Ravikant calls permissioned. You need someone's permission to borrow their time, which requires "incredible leadership" and carries high risks of interpersonal conflict. Think about your workplace and people's attitude toward their managers, executives, and investors, and you'll empathize. It can be a fragile way to scale.

In the tutoring example, imagine the tutor demanding $20 an hour, or poaching your students at $25 an hour or suing you for not providing benefits. These risks will only escalate as the company scales. Employees can sue you and even bring the company to the ground with office politics. On top of that, labor leverage provides little flexibility to scale back in the downtimes. Yet people often use labor leverage because it's easy to get started, and scales, even if it's slower and hairier than other forms of leverage like capital.

Capital Leverage

Capital leverage, in the context of our discussion, is not exclusive to financial leverage (or usage of debt), but refers to all possible leverage generated by capital from these characteristics:

- **Capital is semi-rivalrous:** In contrast to time, a single dollar can be simultaneously used by several people. That happens through credit. Let's say you deposit $100K into the bank. That bank will retain $10K, and lend out $90K. You then go to an investor pointing to your $100K balance and say you want to borrow $80K to buy a company. Under this straightforward scenario, your initial $100K enabled the bank to have $10K, some stranger $90K, and you $80K. Once you buy the company, the previous owners will have another $80K, deposit it into a bank, and a similar cycle will repeat.

   So, the same dollar can be utilized by multiple people, and even more when you incorporate financial instruments and strategies like securities lending, margin loans, and derivatives. As a reference point to just how much a single dollar is used, Ray Dalio, in his discussion on *How the Economic Machine Works*, noted about $50 trillion was credit and $3 trillion was money[8] in the United States. That's what I mean by *semi*-rivalrous. The implication that follows is that capital can be *positive* sum in contrast to time, which is inherently zero-sum.

- **Capital is permissioned:** Capital, like labor, requires permission of someone else to let you manage their capital if you want to use it as a form of leverage. So, it doesn't necessarily require ownership, but stewardship to manage capital.
- **Capital is fungible:** Capital is fungible and can trade itself for labor or capabilities like that of factories. It's the common currency of exchange. Capital can substitute your own labor too, for example, by buying stocks of NVIDA to capture the upside, instead of working there.

Capital is a complex instrument that is highly fungible, meaning it can provide you leverage in endless ways from hedge funds borrowing unowned stocks for investing through short selling, to companies converting capital to secure labor leverage of employees, to replacing said labor by buying manufacturing plants. The important aspect I make note of here is that capital *de-couples productivity from your time*, with far faster growth rates and higher natural ceiling than time.

Capital Scales Geometrically Recall the tutoring example from earlier. For every $30 an hour, you had to pay the tutor $15 an hour, or half of your hourly rate. Now imagine instead the next tutor comes along and says $10 an hour is enough. The next says $5 is good, and so on. The more the scale, the cheaper it becomes—diminishing marginal costs, growing in a geometric shape. That's how capital tends to scale.

I saw this dynamic firsthand when working at SoftBank. SoftBank Vision Fund at the time was managing about $100 billion with a few hundred people. By the time I left, SoftBank had reached about $150 billion in assets,[9] part of it from appreciation of our investments, and a part of it from a second fund. But our head count did not increase proportionately. In fact, it remained the same. In contrast, if a consulting firm (which heavily rely on labor leverage) was to double its revenue, it would roughly require doubling the number of labor hours, especially if the prices have hit the upper limit.

Capital Leverage at Scale   One of its pinnacles is BlackRock, which is the largest asset manager in the world, managing $10 trillion of capital as of 2023.[10] The amount of influence they have on companies—including significant voting rights on Fortune100 companies—and even countries as the largest capital allocator in the world is impressive. Yet, BlackRock doesn't own any of that capital. They have authority over that capital because they receive permission to manage it. With that authority alone, they are able to hold incredible influence in the world and generate billions[11] in revenue.

Trade-offs of Scaling with Capital Leverage   Capital leverage scales faster and farther than labor leverage, but it's a lot harder to get started with. Unless you're using your own capital, managing capital comes with significant costs. Aside from legal requirements, you need to build credibility for others to trust you with their capital. It's easier to convince someone to work for you than it is to convince someone to manage their life savings, even if arguably, their time is more precious.

More importantly, capital leverage can decline as fast as it scales. Remember that capital leverage is permissioned, meaning someone has given you authority to use it and manage it, but you do not own the capital, unlike labor. If you end up losing credibility on your competence or integrity, people can simply allocate their capital to someone else who will do it better. That's how many hedge funds disappeared overnight during the 2008 financial crisis. So capital scales well, but not as well as the most modern forms of leverage, responsible for rapid wealth generation in our time.

Software and Media Leverage

At the cost of losing some nuance and precision, I'll describe software and media as a single form of leverage, as both base units, code and content, have zero marginal cost.

- **Code and content are non-rivalrous:** A large number of people can consume and use it simultaneously without reducing or damaging the base unit of code and content. Software and content have slightly different behaviors when it comes to this:
  - **Code:** Once code is written to do something, it can be used by others. GitHub, for example, is a repository of open-source projects, containing code to accomplish a certain task. Engineers can use and adapt the code, which is why engineers don't need to reinvent the wheel every time they're coding something new.
  - **Content:** Similarly, the words I've written can be read at the same time by multiple people without damaging the base unit. The restrictions, if any, come from bandwidth of platforms sharing the content, not the base unit itself. Though, intellectual property adds complications in some cases.
- **Code and content are permissionless:** Unlike labor and capital, code and media do not require permission to create. When I crunched numbers as a consultant, I'd script code with Excel VBA to automate redundant tasks. I didn't borrow anyone's time or need someone to allocate capital to do this. I wrote the script, and had the work done. When I started writing online, I wrote whenever I wanted, wherever I wanted, and just about whatever I wanted. There were no gatekeepers.
- **Code and content are fungible:** Like capital, code and content are fungible. For example, code can replace manual labor and create a wide array of functions, which can generate capital—that's the foundation of many tech start-ups. In the case of my book, I now have a long-form media asset made up of words. This base unit can be utilized to create new forms of

written assets. I can break them down for several short-form writing opportunities like tweets, threads, newsletters, and posts. With some creativity, I can transform these base units into other media assets like podcasts and reels.

As an extension of these properties, software and media have probably one of the most conducive base units for *Asymmetric Principles*, especially for the upside. "Stacking odds" naturally happens as these non-exhausted, non-rivalrous assets keep stacking up like a catalog, each adding to the probability of one eventually popping off. "Uncapped upsides without artificial barriers" come into play from their permissionless nature. Code, for example, has exceptional fungibility to replace all sorts of value, including labor and capital—products of top AI companies including OpenAI and the like rely on a bundle of code and data.

Software and Content Scales Exponentially The non-rivalrous with near-zero marginal costs of software and content enable an exponential growth curve at scale. These base unit characteristics make them highly favorable for *Asymmetric Principles*, which embeds the need for rapid growth.

Remember that leverage amplifies impact of what you already have, and doesn't discriminate against the direction. Steve Jobs, the founder of Apple, emphasized the immense power of software leverage, particularly in hiring talented individuals whose work will be amplified by leverage.

> "Most things in life have a dynamic range in which average to best is at most 2:1. For example if you go to New York City and get an average taxi cab driver versus the best taxi cab driver, you'll probably get to your destination with the best taxi driver 30% faster. And an automobile; what's the difference between the average car and the best? So 2:1 is a big dynamic range for most things in life.

> Now, in software, and it used to be the case in hardware, the differ-
> ence between the average software developer and the best is 50:1,
> maybe even 100:1.Very few things in life are like this, but what I was
> lucky enough to spend my life doing, which is software, is like this."[12]

Trade-off of Scaling with Software and Media Leverage   Software and media leverage are exceptionally effective for the scaling
stages of *Asymmetric Principles*. But they take some time to start. Consider the tutoring case we've been using. It's probably faster to hire
one additional tutor than it is to build software good enough to
replace tutors or record digital courses on par with live human tutoring. Even in my start-up, parts of our product were run manually,
until we gained enough conviction to invest the engineering resources
to automate them. If you're scaling massively, it's probably worth
investing in the software and content leverage, but you can see how
the investment to start can be large.

One other point I'll share is the distinction between the base units
and the distribution channels. While base units, code and content, are
permissionless, most distribution platforms are permissioned. They
always have been. It is an open secret that mobile apps are dominated
by the Apple Store and Google Play, criticized for thwarting innovation from their aggressive take rates reaching 30%. Content of all
forms is gated by Instagram, X, TikTok, YouTube, and other regional
players with the authority to punish via algorithm or outright ban
you. Music is also beholden to Spotify, Apple Music, and YouTube
to the point even the largest artists barely have enough bargaining
power to distribute their music. While we haven't touched upon it,
movies, TV shows, and all forms of code and content face similar
issues. Previous technological shifts of the desktop era shared these,
and the future certainly seems that way with a few players owning the
key foundational models of AI.

While the characteristics to scale exist with the base units of code and
content, the extent of its scalability comes from distribution

platforms. This is why there is a large movement not only for freedom of content, but ownership of audience. The permissioned nature of platforms should be factored into the use of these leverages.

Before concluding the section on the types of leverage, I'll briefly discuss *network* and *reputation*. While outside the definition of leverage, they are important enough to mention.

Network and Reputation

"Network and reputation" is a beast of a topic, with several books dedicated to the topic. I'll strictly scope the discussion to a few aspects related to scaling your initial traction. Network is roughly everyone you know, and reputation is roughly what they think of you. Both are important.

In relation to scaling *Asymmetric Principles*, network is essential because the biggest games in the world happen in teams, not individuals: Companies compete against companies, governments compete against governments, and platforms against platforms. By definition, the Super Upside is a big game. At scale, you will be working as a team, because there are only a handful of big games that you can play as a sole individual.

You cannot do or know everything yourself. Network generally solves an informational problem—finding that one niche expert or that one job you're perfect for and so on—in a timely manner. You need both the weak and strong ties of an intentional professional network to play big games. They will allow you to do far more than what you can do on your own, and in reciprocity, you will help your network go farther. The good news, as you saw in Chapter 4, is *Asymmetric Principles* naturally inclines people to be your champions—from givers to takers.

Reputation is different from network, because it's informed by your actions that either appreciate or depreciate your social currency.

It's what Ray Dalio would call the *believability* principle, placing greater weight in the opinions of people with proven track records of expertise in their space. That extends to beyond expertise, but really every observable action of yours. Reputation can work magic that short-circuits arduous processes with your name. When it comes to scaling *Asymmetric Principles*, you'll realize reputation will become increasingly important and tied to your name. Here's what I mean.

Many careers can get away with perpetually *borrowing* reputation, but *Asymmetric Principles* requires you to build your own rather quickly. In the early days, most of us borrow reputation and credibility from affiliation with schools, organizations, memberships, and companies. These also often become the basis for friends, colleagues, and mentors to stake their social currency for you. While borrowed reputation is sufficient in many careers, it's too diluted for *Asymmetric Principles*. Sam Altman's reputation doesn't hinge on Y-Combinator. Sundar Pichai's reputation isn't reliant on McKinsey. You can only go so far with borrowed reputation.

Scaling *Asymmetric Principles* will be a sobering experience if you've been conflating your reputation and value with an organization behind you. Within the first few upsides of applying *Asymmetric Principles*, you will be pushed to build your own—for yourself and others—and outgrow borrowed reputation. That means placing your own skin in the game to publicly demonstrate your competence, judgement, and integrity to build reputation tied to your name.

Applying Leverage to Life Decisions

In the scaling phases of *Asymmetric Principles*, you'll start to see structural limitations of systems that built your early upsides and momentum. To go beyond your local maxima, you'll need to slow down and adopt new systems optimized to scale, in order to go faster, farther, and safer toward your Super Upside. Leverage is a powerful system to scale. However, remember that its propensity to amplify outcomes doesn't discriminate direction of outcomes—up or down. That's why it's important to adopt systems of leverage to scale what already works.

Recognize, however, that leverage often comes in a blended form in the real world. When I started my company, I worked with my co-founder to hire people for *labor leverage*. I then raised capital from venture capitalists to further amplify our work, benefiting from *capital leverage*. And, my co-founder wrote code and built the product, which could be infinitely scaled, benefiting from *software leverage*. On that journey, I've borrowed reputation from my investors including Y-Combinator and built my own along the way. In Chapter 7, I isolated impacts of different forms of leverage—labor, capital, software and media, and to some extent network and reputation—and its properties for a precise use of leverage. Every tool has trade-offs, and should be considered in your own situation scaling *Asymmetric Principles*. That's where I want to open the next chapter: how do we consider the trade-offs of systems required for *Asymmetric Principles* with the rest of our lives?

Throughout the chapters in Part II, I accentuated both the necessity of using systems and the *trade-offs* of adopting one system over another. However, we don't adopt one single system in our lives, but a *portfolio* of systems to operate different aspects of our lives. In the next chapter, I'll discuss how different systems can work together to soften the blind spots and strengthen the advantages through intentional portfolio constructions.

8

Thinking in Portfolios

"There are no solutions, only trade-offs"[1]

—Thomas Sowell

Suspended between life and death, lies the Midnight Library—an otherworldly archive of the infinite counterfactuals of your life bound in books, placed in endless bookshelves—brought to life by the author, Matt Haig. The main character, Nora Seed, finds herself lost and broken, drawn to this strange place after a devastating decision to end her life. Each book she touches reveals a different path, shaped by decisions she never made. In every version of her life, she finds herself giving up one precious thing for another.[2]

There is merit in being sober about trade-offs we make—that saying yes to something means saying no to another. Every good comes at a cost—either to you or someone or something else. This has been a recurring theme in Part II, especially in relation to use of systems. In Chapter 5, I put forth that everyone uses systems, and it's a matter of which system in which circumstance. The quality of systems will determine the quality of thousands of decisions translated to compounded outcomes. In Chapter 6, I argued that systems employed by start-ups are optimized to consistently identify upsides. The core principles are to play the right games, build good hypotheses through idea mazes, and run minimally viable experiments iteratively. In Chapter 7, I introduced forms of leverage to take your first upsides and scale it massively, each with their own trade-offs. However, these chapters have examined trade-offs of a single system at a time. In reality, we use multiple systems.

In this chapter, I'll discuss a *portfolio of systems,* which enables you to lean in and out of trade-offs of any single system. That is, I consider intentionally *constructing* types of portfolios as it relates to your career and life more broadly. In the first half of this chapter, I'll discuss why you might consider a portfolio at all. In the latter half, I discuss how *Asymmetric Principles* can fit in with the rest of your overall life portfolio.

Everyone Hates Foxes

Gazing out my Brutalist concrete dorm—a jarring intrusion in the beautiful meadows of Wolfson College—I paused mid-sip of my bitter espresso, watching a fox tear into a squirrel. Not just any squirrel. It was the one my flatmates and I had semi-adopted as a pet. I could see why everyone hated the fox, even before I picked up my copy of *The Hedgehog and the Fox* by Isaiah Berlin, the founder of my college at Oxford.

Berlin starts with a quote from the Greek poet Archilochus: "The fox knows many things, but the hedgehog knows one big thing." Berlin suggests that there are two broad types of writers and thinkers: hedgehogs, who view the world with a single paradigm; and foxes, who view the world from a wide variety of ideas that do not necessarily come together as a single, cohesive, paradigm. In the first few pages of the book, he shares a caveat that it's not intended to be intellectually rigorous. *"Of course, like all over-simple classifications of this type, the dichotomy becomes, if pressed, artificial, scholastic, and ultimately absurd."*[3] He then proceeds to write close to 100 pages from this single motif to determine if Leo Tolstoy was a hedgehog or a fox. I'll save you the read and give you Berlin's conclusion: Tolstoy was a fox who wanted to be a hedgehog.

Since then, parallels have been drawn from the metaphor in a variety of disciplines. When it comes to careers, the two animals symbolize two opposite ends of the spectrum. Do you focus on one thing like a hedgehog, or do you focus on many things like a fox? The reality is that both models of playing the game have track records of success. In my immediate vicinity, I have former colleagues who focused solely on a finance career and built a portfolio of personal assets. Others have taken on multiple titles from founder to coach to creator to speaker and built a personal conglomerate. The titans of our industry also seem to share a mixed bag of the fox and hedgehog strategy.

No Love for the Fox

Yet, in almost every narrative, the fox always seems to receive the short end of the stick. Jim Collins, in his book *Good to Great*, suggests that truly great companies have characteristics of a hedgehog—simple and focused, rather than complex and sophisticated.[4] Altos Ventures, a multibillion-dollar fund that invested in unicorn start-ups like Coupang, Toss, and Roblox, has an entire section on their website ". . . many people are not so pleased when they first hear that we regard them as Hedgehogs. But it is perhaps the best compliment we can give."[5] Even the ancients disliked the fox. In the famed Aesop's Fable, *The Fox and The Cat*, the fox brags about all the skills he has to avoid dangers to the cat but meets the fate of being eaten alive by hounds, while the cat escapes by climbing the tree.[6] Some even think breaking into other fields *after* succeeding in one area is a stretch. Jimmy Carr, a world-class comedian, in an interview said, "I'm not sure I approve of portfolio sort of working. . . . I'm doing it 100% of the time, and you think you can compete 50% of the time. All the best, let's see how you do."[7] The moral of these stories is clear: there is valor in unwavering focus and commitment to one thing. Many leaders echo this sentiment, and point to the paths of success in one area before they break into different fields.

Now, I don't intend to mischaracterize their stance with a straw man. Many concede there are some merits of being a fox, offering several caveats to accompany their opinion. But on balance, there seems to be preference for the hedgehog.

If everyone hates foxes, should we even bother thinking about a portfolio?

A Case to Be Foxy

The fox wasn't always so hated. Dismissing the foxy approach would be a shame, as so much has come from foxy entrepreneurs, inventors, and polymaths throughout history. Perhaps the most well documented era was during the Renaissance, when everyone was doing everything—math, science, philosophy, art, literature—at once. In that period, there was an emphasis on interdisciplinary learnings, with proliferation of polymaths that excelled in many disciplines. Rene Descartes, known for his famed *cogito ergo sum* (I think therefore I am) in metaphysics also contributed to geometry, through Cartesian coordinates, allowing for algebraic representation of geometric shapes. If Leonardo Da Vinci was alive today, I imagine he'd have socials that looked something like this (Figure 8.1).

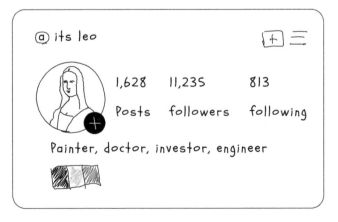

Figure 8.1   Da Vinci's Link in Bio

Others, like Francis Bacon, Galileo Galilei, and many more, held different interests and expertise at once. In fact, the Renaissance was such a prominent era of intersectional innovation and advancement that there is a term called "The Medici Effect," referring to the Medici family that created a legacy through cross-disciplinary innovation.[8]

As biased as I may be with my own portfolio approach, I do not think the Medici Effect applies only in the past. In fact, portfolios can be constructed to cut through the primary critique of dispersing intensity and focus competing at the top of your field. There are two primary reasons people decide to build a portfolio both in industries and careers: diversification and synergies.

Diversifying a $47 Billion Crash

Recall from Chapter 7 that leverage is a multiplier. Leverage doesn't discriminate against good or bad impacts; it's not for or against your interest. That means it can accelerate downward, too. As the legendary investor Warren Buffet of Berkshire Hathaway said:

> "My partner [Charlie Munger] says there are three ways a smart person can go broke: liquor, ladies, and leverage. Now the truth is—the first two he just added because they started with L—it's leverage."[9]

The most dramatic case of downward leverage I've witnessed up close was the $47 billion crash in 2019. Though I was not directly involved in the deal, I had a front row seat to see WeWork crumble from a $47 billion value in 2019 down to almost zero in a matter of months after failed attempts at going public. By 2023, they filed for bankruptcy.[10] WeWork had all the leverage in the world—billions in capital, world-class talent, scalable technology, and a considerable reputation in the entire start-up world. Yet they failed extremely quickly as soon as the direction of leverage pointed in the wrong direction. WeWork is not an isolated incident in the start-up world. Every year, start-ups rise and fall from billions in value plummeting to nothing. Fast, a one-click checkout company, raised more than $100 million and closed down a year later.[11]

Essentially, leverage creates a "bigger you are, the harder you fall" effect. Capital leverage, which is specifically what Buffet referred to, shares these characteristics. Greensill was another failed investment I saw while I was at SoftBank. The company was once a multibillion-dollar trade finance company that provided working capital on collateralized receivables or factoring. Factoring, put simply, works like the following: let's say you sold $100 worth of products, but you won't receive the money until 60 days from the day of the sale. But you need the money now, not two months from now. Greensill would provide liquidity, say $95 today, and take your invoice as their own to receive the full $100 60 days from now. And for a while this was scaling well.

But when capital leverage multiplied in the wrong direction, it only took a week for the multibillion-dollar company to tumble. On March 1, 2021, the trigger started with insurance companies refusing to renew coverage on Greensill's leverage. On March 3, Greensill started defaulting on debts. By March 8, Greensill filed for insolvency. And losses from Greensill's leveraged downward spiral was one of the first pieces of Jenga that led to the toppling of Credit Suisse in 2023, which was ultimately acquired by UBS for pennies on the dollar.[12]

Despite these spectacular downfalls, SoftBank is very much alive today. Why? Because of its own diversified portfolio that softens the blows.

Defensive Diversification   Diversification is the first, and probably the most well-known, benefit of portfolios. Portfolio is an unintended consequence of making many investments, but not all portfolios are necessarily diversified. Creating a balanced, diversified portfolio takes intention. A defining characteristic of a diversified portfolio is that the components are at least partly *uncorrelated* or *negatively correlated*. Investing in an oil company and an airline is a textbook example of negatively correlated investments. Roughly, when the cost of the oil goes up, the value of the oil company goes up, but the value of the airline—sensitive to cost of jet fuel—falls. It's a defense against a single failure leading to systemic failure. That's also why SoftBank survived big losses like WeWork. Effects of diversification kicked in, along with impact of outsized returns that outweigh the errors of venture investments still hold—though to a lesser degree than early stage VCs, who can be wrong many more times.

Similar benefits of diversifications hold in terms of careers. Over the last decade, I've built my own unique career portfolio of experiences, skills, and networks to be resilient. For example, if my start-up were to die tomorrow, it wouldn't be infeasible to return to working as a technology investor. If the entire tech industry crumbles, it wouldn't be out of the question to find a role in consulting or even policy. If all the white-collar work was replaced by AI, it is not unthinkable for me to return to my flight school to earn my instructor's certificate and teach aviation to aspiring pilots. Would I enjoy any one of these scenarios happening? Not one bit. But I'd likely survive. At the risk of sounding like that fox about to be eaten alive by hounds, I built a portfolio of systems that allow me to survive when downsides are realized. In fact, I'd argue that if you don't split *any* focus and attention across uncorrelated things, then a single event can take you out. But diversification isn't just a defensive tactic for when things go wrong. It's an offensive tactic to drive you forward.

Offensive Diversification   In 1966, Abraham Maslow famously said, "I suppose it's tempting, if the only tool you have is a hammer, to treat everything as if it were a nail."[13] When you have several tool-kits, you can be far more creative in any work you do. In fact, taking frameworks and systems from one context to another allowed me to advance faster when I started something new. When I first started writing online, I applied the start-up toolkit from Chapter 6 to find traction, using adaptations like "writer-market fit" and "content-market fit." I grew to thousands of followers with minimal effort. In fundraising for my own start-up, I leveraged skills I learned as an investor, including projection models and generating just enough proof points, which allowed me to raise on a pitch deck without a product or team. I'm not cherry-picking a few stories from my life here.

In a longitudinal study, Bernice Eiduson studied characteristics and behaviors that contributed to the researchers' scientific success. Eiduson followed 40 leading scientists including the Nobel Prize winner, and one of my favorite authors, Richard Feynman. She measured 50 variables of which 32 had statistical significance and summarized her findings in the book *Scientists: Their Psychological World*.[14] In his TED Talk "A Powerful Way to Unleash Your Natural Creativity," Tim Harford expanded on this study, sharing that the "most enduringly creative scientists switched topics 43 times in their first 100 research papers."[15]

Another commonly known example is interplay between music and math. The music legend John Coltrane used mathematics to create complex musical structures in jazz. A famed example the Circle of Fifths, a diagram sketching out relationships between notes in a spatial diagram, and creating his own visual representation, "Coltrane's Circle," that shows the harmonic relationship between notes and transitional entries.[16] He used these techniques in his album *Giant Steps,* which involved harmonic progression with movement in thirds, again known as Coltrane changes. Use of mathematics in music traces back centuries from Johann Sebastian Bach's sophisticated use of counterpoint captured in *The Art of Fugue* theory[17] to Iannis Xenakis, who pioneered use of stochastic processes in music, incorporating probability theory to determine progression in music.[18]

Diversifying portfolio isn't just to minimize fatal losses from failures, but can play an offensive role. Splitting your focus doesn't necessarily mean being less productive or detracting from your core activities. Offensively diversifying enables crosspollination of skills and innovations to elevate your entire portfolio to compete with the hedgehogs even at the top of their field.

Double-Dipping Synergies: Work Once, Win Twice

Synergies is the second, less appreciated, benefit of building a portfolio. In my view, it's the aspect that counters the critique of spreading yourself too thin. Why? Because synergy allows you to double-dip on your single efforts to push forward your entire portfolio. There are two flavors of synergies I'll share with the example of Apple.

The first type of synergy is collectively increasing the value of the portfolio or "the whole is greater than the sum of its parts." Anyone who's been sucked into the Apple ecosystem will have realized this—after it's too late to switch over. The iPhone is great. But have you tried pairing it with the Mac? The first time I learned I can copy text from my phone and paste on my Mac was a delight—literally "delighted the customer." The fact that I can airdrop files to my iPad seamlessly made my life easier. Every time I buy a new Apple device, the iCloud becomes more valuable, because I can access files from any one of them. For every additional Apple product I buy, the more valuable the ecosystem becomes for me. That's the first flavor.

The second type of synergy is collectively decreasing the cost of the portfolio or "the cost is lower than the sum of its parts," through the utilization rate of your efforts. Imagine Apple with just a single product—the iPhone. Consider the investment needed to promote and market the iPhone. In contrast, with a portfolio of products, promotions and marketing raises all boats for products. The cost of branding stays relatively the same, but the cost on a per product basis falls dramatically. And Apple crushed it, becoming the "the world's most valuable brand name" surpassing a value of $1 trillion dollars.[19] Synergy is powerful.

Both types of synergies can be achieved by intentionally building your life portfolio. Again, I'll walk through a narrow, career-related hypothetical case, which is easily actionable. Imagine you're working on three things concurrently:

- Writing your PhD thesis on content virality on social media platforms
- Launching a personal YouTube channel on marketing
- Building a social media marketing company

If you laid out all the tasks you'd need to do for each of these pursuits, you'll notice that a considerable number of them coincide. By doing what you were going to do anyway with one task, you'd contribute to the two other pursuits simultaneously. Essentially, you're double-dipping on a single task.

Let's say a part of your thesis research is analyzing the top 1,000 most viral YouTube videos to build a set of predictive variables (which is something Mr. Beast, the most subscribed YouTuber, did in his teenage years,[20] except you'd be paid to do it while progressing your degree) on how videos go viral. These learnings help you build your YouTube channel for virality and design a framework for your marketing company. That's one flavor of synergy—reducing the collective cost of the portfolio to less than the sum of its parts.

At the same time, growth of these pieces will increase the portfolio value beyond the sum of its parts. For example, your YouTube channel can be used to directly test your PhD hypotheses on virality, and its outcome—viral or not—can be used to inform both your research and your marketing company. When the videos do go viral eventually, they become a case study and a natural sales funnel for your marketing company. At the same time, a PhD stipend would be financing you to be running these experiments. The obvious trade-off of having many tasks coincide is increase in correlations and reduction in diversification—so if the entire creator space was to tumble, the risk of complete failure is higher. However, the point stands that portfolios can be constructed in a way to maximize synergies.

By the way, this hypothetical is not a far-fetched idea. Many of my former colleagues building start-ups in the creator economy have become creators. By creating content, they became intimately familiar with the problems to solve for their customers, naturally improving the product. Their creator content became a sales engine to attract more creators, which in turn grew their own creator profile and the product. While some have been more successful than others in such a strategy, strategically building a portfolio for synergies can work well.

Doing one thing—just like the hedgehog—can effectively push forward several portfolios at once. Not only does it push it forward, but each creates a loop that reinforces the growth of one another, until they build their own momentum. It's these synergies that enable foxes to be working on several things, yet deliver outcomes that are just as good, and at times better, than the single focus of hedgehogs.

So, Hedgehog or Fox?

Should you be a hedgehog or a fox? I'd start by saying that these are metaphors, and probably not hard rules to live by. Even Berlin himself noted it shouldn't be taken so seriously *"the dichotomy becomes, if pressed, artificial, scholastic, and ultimately absurd."* If you try to practically live by one, you'll see it'll become complex quite quickly. For example, is being a hedgehog working on only one thing during your lifetime or a few years at a time? Is being a fox working on many things sequentially or only simultaneously? Is research in both ancient Greek poetry and history considered foxy or is it classified as a hedgehog studying ancient Greece? Is doing one thing at a time sequentially a foxy hedgehog or a hedgehogy fox? How many things are too much or too little in a portfolio? What happens if doing one thing entails doing many things, like a VC who invests across sectors? Don't take it as an absolute.

Astute readers may have noticed that I haven't actually answered the question beyond "it depends." That was intentional. This entire section has been about trade-offs. My goal was to share my understanding of the trade-offs and strategies to building your portfolio. The decision falls on you. That said, I will share what's worked for me as a reference point, which is a cycle of transitioning between fox and hedgehog behavior every few years—like an hourglass on its side. I have a wide array of interests, which narrow, until it widens again.

In my freshman year of college, I joined six student clubs, ran for student politics, started side projects, taught aviation to cadets, and served a church. By the time I graduated, I narrowed my activities down to two things. In my early career as a consultant, I again joined a variety of committees and groups. At SoftBank, I focused only on investing and supported just one social impact initiative for underrepresented founders in the start-up ecosystem. In my first semester at Oxford, I grew my interests again, joining the debating union, the college rowing team, and readings in ethics. Now as a start-up founder, my exclusive focus is my company, with writing a few hours a month as a way to de-stress my life and develop my thinking.

Both approaches, having many eggs in many baskets, and watching a single basket carefully, have worked well for me in different stages of my life. The important thing is not whether a hedgehog or fox is inherently better or worse but recognizing the trade-offs and adapting the one that works for you. Great, animals are cool, but how does all of this fit in the context of *Asymmetric Principles*?

Life Portfolio and Asymmetric Principles

The focal point of this book has been about identifying, realizing, and scaling outsized returns through *Asymmetric Principles*. But opportunities skewed in your favor represent a small fraction of opportunities in life, especially in the early days of applying these principles. It would be disingenuous to pretend that reading a few thousand words will suddenly fill your life with perfect asymmetric opportunities. On the contrary, most things, I've observed, have *symmetrical* risk to reward ratios, and often have far less variance than asymmetric opportunities. That's analogous to the financial sector. Most institutions allocate less than 5% of their portfolio to highly variant asymmetric opportunities, or *alternative investments* like venture capital. Having an entire portfolio that consistently relies on outrageously outsized wins like venture capital is an exception, not the rule.

Similarly, only a few opportunities in your life portfolio will initially have outsized returns when you start out—much like how I started on the farms of Manitoba. Over time, as compounding effects of *Asymmetric Principles* kick in, more of your portfolio will be asymmetric. The practical question is how the rest of your life fits in with *Asymmetric Principles* on that journey. With that context, I'll tighten up the scope of "life portfolio" in relation to *Asymmetric Principles* beyond careers.

Your Life Portfolio Determines Asymmetry

Whether you've been intentional or not, you've constructed a life portfolio. What you'll have noticed is that portfolio construction strategy like diversification and synergies isn't determined by any one opportunity, but directly in relation to the rest of the portfolio. Now, "life portfolio" sounds like a hollow concept that can mean anything from a collection of relationships to experiences to emotions, a type of vagueness that can seem distasteful. But whatever way you slice and dice the composite, the point I'm driving stands: Opportunities within definitional scopes of *Asymmetric Principles* are highly determined by the rest of your life portfolio composites.

In Chapter 2, I pointed out that variance and probability of possible future scenarios are objective, but the impact of those outcomes is subjective. That is, the same range of outcomes that's great for one person may be catastrophic for another, depending on the rest of their portfolio. In contrast, a huge upside for one person may not be out-sized enough to make the bets for another person. These differences in life portfolio positions are why, in a financial sense, I wouldn't blindly copy the next investment made by Warren Buffet or Ray Dalio. Their investment objectives, risk appetite, and access are very different from mine. And what may be an asymmetric opportunity for one person may not be one for another depending on the cir-cumstances, obligations, and values. It's something I've learned grow-ing up from a modest background.

In 2015, I was offered a $10,000 signing bonus from my first full-time job. I was 20 at the time, and took that offer with a huge sense of relief. It was the first time my net worth was above zero. Accepting a job at a consulting firm may look like a traditional path, but given the rest of my life portfolio—having no network growing up on a farm, no work experience, and no financial stability for my family—taking that traditional consulting job *was* applying the *Asymmetric Principles*. Building a safety net with a high salary at a renowned company and gaining experience gave me maneuverability to start raising my floors and uncapping my upside in other parts of my life. Eventually, more and more opportunities in my life became asymmetric.

But even back in 2015, many of my peers said, "there is no downside of doing a start-up"—in the best case, your start-up will change the world, and the worst case, you gain start-up experience, and maybe live on your friends' couches for a few months until you get another job. That may have been true for some people, but it wasn't for me. Had I started my company then, the decision would have been outside my definition of *Asymmetric Principles*, and what I'd describe as reckless behavior. My point is to be sober about constraints and the rest of your life portfolio.

My primary constraint was a lack of financial safety and, to some degree, a lack of a network and exposure. For you, constraints may be related to health, language, interpersonal conflicts (or lack thereof), trauma, addictions, or other nuanced battles you may be fighting alone. Everyone has to start somewhere, and having a stable foundation allowed me to elevate the rest of my life portfolio that naturally make the same opportunities favorably asymmetric. As *Asymmetric Principles* raises your floor and uncaps your upsides, your position to take favorable asymmetric opportunities will improve. In the earliest days, the practical step is balancing the rest of your career and life while applying *Asymmetric Principles* in small ways.

Looking back to my own highly constrained life portfolio growing up, I've thought hard about the design of *Asymmetric Principles*, so anyone can get started at any point—even as small as 15 minutes. But it took time to position the rest of my life to be able to take bigger asymmetric swings. In retrospect, there were a number of things I could've done to get there faster. I'll share a few things in the next section.

A Few Things That Tilt Luck in Your Favor

The advice I received over and over early in my life was to first, figure out "what I want," and *then* work backward to reach that goal. Well, the practical implication is that it can take a lifetime to answer the existential question of "why am I here?" Even today, I don't know with certainty exactly what I want or where I'm going, even in the narrow bounds of career. I have a general hunch based on what I enjoy and what I'm good at. I'm following a path of *growth* through

Asymmetric Principles that'll lead me to the Super Upside. Whether you're still figuring yourself out, or your life portfolio constraints prevent you from taking big swings, I'll share a few tactical things that tend to attract luck. I'm going to stay away from unobservable virtues like curiosity, kindness, or integrity (only you truly know), and stick to observable, objective pieces of the portfolio you can prioritize as you figure things out. It's the sort of things that'll probably give a leg up in whatever you end up doing, and certainly set you up to have more asymmetric opportunities in your life.

Free Up Brain Space

There is considerable literature on the impairment of general cognitive abilities from brain space overload. In the 2013 study *Poverty Impedes Cognitive Functions*, researchers found that chronic worrying of finances leaves less mental bandwidth available for other tasks, making people "poorer" in cognitive resources from what they call a bandwidth tax. One way it was tested was with sugarcane farmers in India, who typically receive the bulk of their income once a year immediately after harvest. Farmers took cognitive tests like Raven's Progressive Matrices and Stroop Tasks under conditions of relatively high financial stress (before pre-harvest) and financial ease (post-harvest) with the difference in results, equivalent to a 13-point reduction in IQ.[21] Declutter your brain.

Financials are not the only worries that occupy the mind with micro decisions that drain your energy. For some, that can mean resolving relationship conflicts, focusing on health, or building savings. As you're building your foundation and direction, prioritize securing brain space.

Watch the Waves

People with average skills, effort, and luck who *ride* the wave seem to outperform people with exceptional skills, effort, and luck who *fight* it. If you're learning to catch one, surfers will tell you to start by watching the waves.

One signal is the *rate of change*. Rapid changes generally mean waves are coming. Typically, that manifests in growth or a shift in public opinion and laws. For example, the Generative AI market, which is a subset of the AI market, has exploded from about $14 billion in 2020 to estimated more than $137 billion by 2024 according to Bloomberg. In four years, it grew by about 870%, trending to be well more than a $900 billion market by 2030.[22] Even from a tech perspective, the rate of improvement in model sizes and capabilities is moving at a frightening pace. Another signal is the sheer size of the wave. There was more than $30 trillion in assets under management related to sustainability in 2022, and it is expected to grow to $40 trillion by 2030.[23] At some point, they will need to deploy that capital and invest in someone. The market is just so huge and growing at a steady pace. These are the sorts of waves you want to ride.

If you don't know where to start, an imperfect, but workable jumping off point is checking websites of top venture capital funds and see what they're investing in. As much as I don't glorify VCs to be more than they are—capital allocators—their investments are educated guesses or proxies of waves that have already hit or will hit. Generally, earlier stage investors have further outlooks of a decade, and growth stage investors have shorter outlooks of three to five years. Depending on the timeline of your bets, this will matter.

Watching the waves is one reason I pulled the trigger to start my company in 2021. The capital inflow to start-ups and the tech valuations were at all-time highs. Securing capital at zero-interest rate environment in a rapidly growing creator economy were all waves on the rise. I rode those waves and raised my pre-seed round on a deck. No product, no revenue, no customers, just a good idea riding good waves.

In the process of building your life portfolio, keep an eye out on the waves.

Building Distribution

Naval Ravikant tweeted "Every single tweet costs nothing and has the potential to reach the entire world. It's the best lottery ever made."[24]

Distribution is an unbelievably democratized superpower. Almost anyone can build some sort of audience in some niche. Whether that's through writing or videos or communities or other opportunities, having direct access to a large number of people who listen to your voice is a powerful piece of your portfolio that will serve you in almost any path you take.

You want to be a writer? Publishers will look at your following. You want to be a musician? Record labels look at your following. You want to sell your own products? Customers need to believe you. You want to build a product? You have your initial users who are willing to test your bad product and give you early feedback.

Even in the context of careers, one of my predictions is that distribution will start to be included on CVs and resumes in the future of work. Imagine a small athletic wear company with 10 employees, each with 100,000 followers interested in athletic wear. That's a million in reach right off the bat. Among equally skilled candidates, why wouldn't companies pick the people who have built a following and serve as early users of any new product? With improving efficiencies from tech, and now AI, these teams will likely run on smaller, tighter groups who can directly contribute to growth—there will be fewer places to hide. But even if you don't agree with my prediction, building an audience has considerable positive side effects that can help in whatever you do.

For one, it often requires you to produce, which puts you in the overwhelming minority with an edge. Think about what proportion of people produce versus consume, whether its media, code, product, or art. And as you produce, you'll start to see the quality of your consumption improve. It's a different kind of reading when you have an intention of writing. It's a different type of listening when you have aspirations to write music. It's a different kind of watching when you intend to create the content. Another is independence. When you have your own audience, you don't need to ask for permission from platforms. Your audience chose you. That, of course, can lead directly into being independent from employers or gatekeepers. If you recall in my scenario forecasts of starting to write online, a large part of it was building my own distribution. That way, I wouldn't be at the mercy of publishers. I'd have the option of publishing on my own with people who want to read my writing.

Providing Leverage

In a world where everyone is told they are the main character, becoming skilled at providing leverage to others will make you extremely attractive. It's also a good starting point for building professional relationships. In Chapter 7, I discussed how powerful leverage can be, and it follows that everyone else wants leverage. You can stand out by providing people with leverage. I've seen some people falsely equating providing leverage to being exploited. Providing leverage out of volition is not exploitation. In fact, if you can provide leverage for a lot of people at scale—like the most successful companies in the world—people will fight to work with you.

Shopify is a great example of this. Shopify is a Canadian unicorn that provides software for online sellers to procure and sell products online, providing significant *leverage* for more than 2 million merchants. In 2023, Shopify generated $7.1 billion in revenue. At the same time, online sellers generated $235 billion on Shopify.[25] That means, for every dollar generated by the merchant, Shopify generated about three cents. That's a 33× leverage for merchants. I don't think Shopify was exploited. Similar success stories are found everywhere from Upwork, enabling freelancers to find work and be paid for a fraction of the earnings; or Airbnb, providing homeowners a way to generate income for a fee; or PayPal and Stripe, allowing merchants to receive payments from all over the world for a fraction of the value created.

Applied to individual lives, provide leverage to your company, your manager, and your peers while protecting yourself. See what happens. Once enough people line up to work with you for your leverage, you can choose who to work with. Learning to provide leverage sustainably is a great piece of your portfolio to build in almost every circumstance. Anchor your value to how much value you create, not what someone else is making.

Don't Be Ugly

When I shared my plans to write this section, a friend of mine jokingly told me I'd get cancelled. Well, I've rolled the dice. Whether we like it or not, there are a considerable number of studies that document that presentation matters. For example, do I, as a 5'7" man, get annoyed that I would've statistically made an extra $166,000 more over my career had I been 6 feet tall?[26] Yes. Absolutely furious. I could protest that it's discrimination or accuse people of being superficial. I could pronounce with temerity that I'm not a statistic. But it doesn't change the propensity of people ascribing a premium on height, and selective generosity is a prerogative.

Like height, a number of studies show biases toward physical attributes, and really, physical attractiveness. I'll start with the most politically incorrect one, and that's our faces and bodies. To say that attractiveness is entirely socially constructed, in my view, is a stretch. Aesthetics is a field of study dedicated to understanding measures of beauty, from symmetry, proportions, and balance that consistently predict perception of beauty. Studies have shown that even babies smiled more at prevailing attractive faces, consistently across cultures.[27] Another aspect is odor. Simply bad body odor, often driven by genetic differences, leads to negative perception on completely unrelated areas including:[28]

- Less competence, reliability, and employability in interviews
- Less social, cooperative, and unpleasant in team environments
- Less sexually attractive

In contrast, having a pleasant odor such as a perfume positively impacted mood, the perception of being reliable, and a propensity to help others. I backed these up with references to studies, but I don't think we need a huge burden of proof here. If it smells like death every time someone opens their mouth to talk to you or simply standing beside them makes you nauseous, you probably wouldn't want to be around them. Same thing applies with varying degrees of discriminatory behavior based on physical attractiveness.

My conclusion is not that we should adhere to ridiculous beauty standards set by super models. But at a minimum, it is worth putting in effort on your appearance and how you are received by others. Ideally, we can be attractive human beings to be around—both inside and out. To be clear, I'm not telling anyone to do anything, but sharing observable, probabilistic trade-offs of presenting yourself in one way or another. The good news is, unlike my height, most of you have significant control on your presentation. Even luck favors beauty.

These few things are not precise, but that's expected for broad applicability. From a retrospective view, these are areas I would have worked on under constraints to position myself for better access to asymmetric opportunities. That, along with applying *Asymmetric Principles* to elevate my floors and uncap my upsides until most of my life portfolio consists of opportunities defined by *Asymmetric Principles*. But I'll stress that *Asymmetric Principles* is still just one part of your life portfolio that truly matter.

Life Is More Than Productivity

Late 2018 was the first time I didn't have an official title tied to a plastic ID. I was briefly in between leaving Oliver Wyman and joining

SoftBank. Whenever I went to a professional gathering, I found myself looking for words during the awkward, but obligatory pleasantries with strangers. Immersion in a culture where people are called by their titles, at least in professional settings, didn't help (in Korea, people refer to you by your last name and title, like North America does with doctors—Dr. Kang—but with many other titles like attorney Kang, author Kang, chef Kang, founder Kang, that extends to even corporate titles like manager Kang). A minor abstraction from the symptom of reducing myself by "what I do" shows a disturbing aspect of linking identity with some kind of productivity.

Social norms could have us describe ourselves by our taxonomy, our hobbies, food preferences, familial relationships, emotions, or a variety of other categories. To some, it can almost seem strange to be fixated on production as the source of identity. Yet, the primary mode of how we introduce ourselves is tied to what we produce. There is probably a selection bias among my readers to have that same propensity to prioritize career over many other aspects in life. That comes at a cost.

When introducing the concept of scenario forecasts to sample a few of infinite outcomes, I used the descriptor "within bounds of reasonable probabilities." Despite considerable effort forecasting and flooring the downsides, unforeseen events outside the range of outcomes in our mental model can occur. When I finished raising funding for my company, I did not predict the immediate interest rate spikes or tech valuation crashes or the bank runs. To a much more extreme extent, victims of war in recent years probably didn't incorporate such tragic events in their life plans and decisions.

These are lessons told even in the realms of fiction. The entire premise of the movie *Me Before You* is a successful man hit by a motorcycle that leads to paralysis. Unexpected health issues, deaths, relationship fallouts, or financial turmoil outside the range of what I perceive to be bounds of reasonable probability can occur. To use the words of

Nicholas Nassim Taleb, these are Black Swan events. Investors survive losses outside the bounds of reasonable probabilities because they've set up a diversified portfolio.

While Chapter 8 has primarily scoped portfolios in context of careers, the benefits of diversification and synergies extend beyond productivity to the life portfolio. How we construct our life portfolio will determine how we survive and even thrive. Over-indexing on one composite can be dangerous, because if that one thing doesn't work out, it can cause *systemic failures*. For example, if I have a career setback, my friends, family, health, hobbies, and spirituality will help me recover from shock and get back on my feet. I've picked on career, because it's the one I'm most prone to prioritizing, but risks of over-indexing hold true for other values. Some people probably are overly invested in romantic relationships, families, or spirituality at the cost of other important values, as the fictional character from the beginning of this chapter, Nora Seed, also realized at the *Midnight Library* going through counterfactuals of her life.

Life often requires more than a single dimension. A fulfilling career, meaningful relationships, reliable health, and sense of purpose are all things that matter. Time, focus, and attention are all scarce resources, which must be allocated across all aspects of life that are valuable, not just asymmetric opportunities. Everyone has different order of importance of values in their lives—from careers to family to love to experience to freedom to hobbies and beyond. I'm not going to prescribe which values ought to be more important than others. You will make your own determination. But there are a few characteristics I keep in mind.

- ■ Order of operations matter. Whether I invest in relationships or experience or skill building, the value of my investment compounds over time. The timing of my investment matters. For example, relationships nurtured in my 20s will probably be wildly different than relationships I start in my 60s. You can't cheat time.

- Some values are more fragile than others. If I lose my job, I can, with reasonable probability, get another one. If I break my health or relationships, it's much harder to fix or substitute.
- Values have expiration dates. Everything I value probably has an expiration date, including the time spent with my loved ones. As such, the priority of values will continue to be in flux with the passage of time.

Asymmetric Principles is not independent of your life, but in fact, entirely dependent on it. Its impact is determined by how you've positioned yourself with your life portfolio. Prescriptions on how to live your life escape the scope of this book, but survival certainly matters in sustainably hitting your Super Upside. In this sense, it seems that while hedgehogs may be favored in the realm of careers, the foxes shouldn't be so hated when it comes to building components of life.

With that in mind, I conclude Part II of the book. Applying *Asymmetric Principles* is about adopting systems, from good hypotheses and experiments that lead to tractions, appropriate use of leverage types to scale beyond structural limits, and portfolio constructions to balance with the rest of your life. The next chapter, which will kick off Part III, is about sustainably applying *Asymmetric Principles* with measures to avoid the central point of failure of all systems: You.

PART III

When Rubber Meets the Road

In Part I, I introduced the basic idea of asymmetry from venture capital investments and shared qualifiers for application to life decisions, which I've summarized as *Asymmetric Principles*. Taking definitions of scenario forecasts—uncapped upsides with a clear path to a non-zero base case that takes you where you want to go, and predictable downside that is floored and tolerable—as the foundation, I've built on ideas of optimizations and compounding factors. I shared how I dogfooded my own framework in several contexts in the last decade, from small 15-minute investments to entire career swings. I share this idea, particularly as a risk-averse individual who grew up with no network, no capital, and no knowledge, and how you can apply it in your life as well. Finally, I shared concerns of conflating predictability of safety, and the instinct to cling to the familiarly tragic over the novel good.

Part II elaborated on these base concepts for a detailed guide on applying *Asymmetric Principles* in personal life decisions. Taking systems as a base unit, I demonstrated that decisions are made with systems, not individual analysis, and it's a matter of which system to adopt. I emphasized the importance of good systems, as decisions compound rapidly—both the good and the bad. In the following chapters, I shared different types of systems optimized for stages of *Asymmetric Principles*. Borrowing from the framework of start-ups, I shared in detail how start-up founders consistently generate upsides, and how such principles apply in the early stages of finding traction. I introduced systems that scale these initial tractions beyond the local maxima, particularly in different forms of leverage, which should be applied in consideration of their trade-offs. Concluding Part II, I discussed integrating multiple systems to lean in and out of trade-offs of any single system, not only for careers, but in life.

As I kick-off Part III, my intention is to preemptively protect readers from predictable stressors that are accentuated when applying *Asymmetric Principles*. Starting with key-person risks and elevated stressors that can lead to systemic failure, I share ways to preemptively address vulnerabilities, including a framework to retain agency and even quit strategically.

9

Avoiding the Single Point of Failure

The world's fastest internet city came to a jarring halt for a few hours in 2022.[1] When I arrived in Seoul to set up our Asia office, I found out that the communication in the entire country was essentially run by a single app: KakaoTalk.

KakaoTalk is a super app with a whopping 93% penetration rate for the population, processing more than a billion messages a day.[2] It serves as the primary communication tool not only for personal messages use but also for governments and corporations. The same app is integrated into every part of life from banking to taxis to gaming to shopping. So, when Kakao's data center caught fire in 2022, the entire country shut down. From just a few hours of outage, the cost to Kakao alone was estimated to be up to 200 billion wons (roughly $150 million), including direct compensations.[3]

A decade earlier in 2011, a similar event shutdown some of the largest social forums like Reddit, Quora, and Foursquare for about three days.[4] Amazon Web Services (AWS) is a cloud computing service that provides computing, storage, and networking services. Elastic Computer Cloud (EC2) specifically provides virtual servers for running applications with an ability to rapidly scale up and down computing resources—an attractive aspect for companies like Reddit where computing resources varied during peak and off-peak times. A network connectivity issue caused a portion of the traffic to be routed incorrectly, leading to an overload on a network. That overload caused Elastic Block Stores (EBS) to lose connectivity to the EC2. The outage lasted for about three days, also causing millions in damages.

If you understood this the first time, great. I certainly didn't. I made a simpler version for myself. Imagine you're at a library. The server is like a librarian. He will bring you specific books and put books away when not in use. He has a small set of books at his desk, but has a nasty habit of throwing away the books when he's done working. EBS is like bookshelves where all books are stored. Data is like books, so every post, comment, like, upload, or share—any information on places like Reddit—is placed somewhere in the bookshelves. Network overload is like a bunch of tourists flooding the library and blocking all the hallways. Now the librarian can't access or organize the bookshelves. When you ask the librarian to help you get the latest version of *The Super Upside Factor*, the hallways are blocked (network overload), and the librarian (EC2 server) cannot fetch the book (data) from the bookshelf (EBS storage). And now you are stuck with the misfortune of not reading this life-changing book.

SPOF and Redundancies

Vulnerabilities from Kakao Corporation and AWS that bring down entire systems are called Single Point of Failure (SPOF). It's the Achillies' heel of systems, but worse, because many variables rely on a single system. Size and sophistication don't seem to help much. At the time of the crash, Amazon had crossed a $100 billion valuation in the public markets in 2011.[5] Even the sophisticated systems of such a large company can be more fragile than you think. Much larger systems like the global financial infrastructure tumbled down in 2008, causing the world to stop. The internet that literally connects the whole world? It's scary that the entire infrastructure of the internet relies on just a few players, including DNS providers. In fact, as systems grow and become more complex, the points of failures, inclusive of SPOFs, increase. So how does one eliminate or minimize SPOFs?

Creating Redundancies

Since the 2011 AWS outage, Amazon accelerated the adoption of distributed cloud infrastructure, spreading out their servers, improving their storage, and perhaps most relevant to prevention, having copies of data across several storage units. Essentially, having copies of the same book across multiple bookshelves in different parts of the library. That way, you can still ask the librarian to find *The Super Upside Factor* even if tourists are blocking the way or bookshelves collapse.

Creating redundancies is a common way to minimize the SPOF across any industry. One of the most prominent examples is in the aviation industry. To nerd out about planes, most of them have several redundancy systems that are mechanical, hydraulic, and electrical. The Airbus A320, for example, has multiple independent wiring systems, so a single short circuit doesn't fry the system. They also have distinct hydraulic systems for critical components, including the flight controls, landing gear, and brakes. On top of that, landing gears have a separate mechanical release in case other systems fail.

A macabre truth is that companies create redundancies of employees as a part of "key-person risk planning." All that means is, can we continue to function if we lost key people involved in work? For large projects during my consulting days, there were restrictions on how many of us could be on the same flight. The morbid rationale behind this, at least in part, was if the plane was to crash, the business could carry on as usual. These sorts of redundancies of employees are not uncommon for professional services, governments, and corporations.

Just like the world's largest, most robust systems can be fragile, our individual systems and life portfolio, despite our best efforts, can be exposed to SPOFs.

Key-Person Risk: You Are Not a Redundancy

Throughout the book, I've drawn parallels between our lives and VCs. But they are exactly that: *parallels*. Yes, there are many lessons to be learned from venture investors who use target skewed bets for 100× returns; or start-up founders who use idea mazes and iterative experiments to identify the first set of upsides; or funds that use leverage to amplify the output; or portfolio managers that generate synergy and diversify risk. But do not make the mistake of reducing yourself to a fund or a start-up or a machine.

You are different, and the one difference is that you are not replaceable. To preempt pushback, there are *aspects* of you that are replaceable. For example, your productivity to your company or team or employees or fans may be replaceable. Even in your family unit, your contribution in tax filing, cooking, cleaning, earning, barbequing, and so on can be replaceable. But *you* are not replaceable to people who care about you. My mom doesn't want another son as a redundancy. My dad doesn't want a Daniel 2.0. with a better operating system. My parents want me. And at the very least, you are irreplaceable to one person, and that's you. So, taking the time to be kind to yourself has value.

As an extension, reflecting on your personal SPOF is a good exercise. My personal rules are: "don't die" and "don't go to jail," and I might even add "don't gamble with my life." That is, try avoiding catastrophic downsides that could permanently destroy your life. I've seen many people inadvertently throw away precious things from critical decisions, including tolerating vices in their lives. Your vices don't come to swallow you when you're at your strongest. They creep up on you when you're at your weakest: overeating happens under stress; procrastination comes with pressure; substance craves come in crisis; relapse occurs during grief; addiction comes back with loneliness. Now, I've stayed away from giving blanket statements on life, as you've seen in Chapter 5 on life goals and again in Chapter 8 on your values. These are questions I refuse to answer for you, as I find that to be irresponsible with no skin in the game for the outcome of your life. At best, I can say take the time to find key vulnerabilities and address them.

What I *can* do is share SPOF in context of *Asymmetric Principles*. Specifically, predictable exposures to stress that are amplified as you apply these principles, and how you can address them to sustainably work toward your Super Upside.

Elevated Stressors

Asymmetric Principles have considerable benefits, but they come with costs. These principles deviate from how most people live their lives. *Asymmetric Principles*, beyond the sheer additional amount of work, will be accompanied by predictably elevated level of stressors, directly impacting your mental well-being, physical health, and relationships. I've included this chapter in the book not because I enjoy talking about emotional subjects, but because addressing stressors is necessary to sustainably apply *Asymmetric Principles*, and guard against your SPOF: You. In this first part of the chapter, I'll discuss some of the non-obvious stressors that escalate the risks of SPOF when applying *Asymmetric Principles*.

Stress from Endless Rejections

The game of *Asymmetric Principles* has a base expectation that *most* of your shots won't work. You'll face a dramatic uptick in both the frequency and magnitude of mental stress. These aren't haphazard shots with a mental attitude of "it is what it is." No, each of your shots at the Super Upside will take considerable effort, from forecasting to idea mazes to iterative experiments, often with your reputation on the line accompanied by considerable emotional attachments. You will have worked day and night with the little resources you have to make it work. Despite such efforts, you'll have to rule out paths, recognize dead ends, and at times, recreate a new idea maze from scratch.

Often, these dead ends manifest themselves through rejections and failures. Trust me, every one of them is accompanied with emotional fatigue. The intellectual understanding that most of your shots won't work out does not give you immunity from disappointment. It doesn't help that these rejections will almost always feel personal.

Rejecting Your Identity   Before starting my pre-seed round, I took pride in having a thick skin. I received tons of rejections from scholarships, grants, and job applications, but pulled through in the past. I knew intellectually that most investor meetings would lead to rejections. But it wasn't fun receiving more than 150 rejections, after hours of investor meetings, building the company, and doing follow-up work. I noticed these rejections hurt more than usual. Why? After reflection, there were two drivers. The first was the concentration of rejections. Receiving rejections a few times here and there is tolerable. Being rejected or, worse, being ghosted, several times a *day* for weeks on end is not. The second was the rejections feeling personal, often like an attack on my identity. Of the two, I'd say the second hit harder.

In the early stages of your *Asymmetric Principles*, everything will feel personal. Companies are funded based on founders and books based on writers. When I was rejected by investors, I shared my personal story of why I started my company and why I'm the right person to build it. It is deeply personal. It can feel like they're rejecting you as a person. In truth, many are to some degree.

Asymmetric Principles requires you to put yourself on the line. It's the same reason that forces you to build your own reputation early on. Scholarships and grad schools require *personal statements*, auditions capture your *personal* interpretations, sharing content publicly requires your *personal* opinions. These personal rejections never really end in *Asymmetric Principles*. Even after raising a successful round for my startup, the brash rejections continued in hiring and sales as well. Decoupling your identity from your work becomes hard, because it is often so closely tied to you as a person.

Stress from Loneliness

Asymmetric Principles demands the little time and resources you have left after sustaining your life. Most times, that involves withdrawing from social life to focus on a mundane cycle to realize your upside. There are *physically* less opportunities to be with others.

On top of that, you'll become less relatable to people around you, because *Asymmetric Principles* requires going against the grain. Things that matter to you may not be pertinent to most people. Taking the narrow category of "creating," consider the proportion of entrepreneurs vs. employees; software builders vs. software users; writers vs. readers; producers vs. listeners; creators vs. viewers; and so on. You'll be joining the minority. Nassim Nicholas Taleb, in his book *Skin in the Game,* describes the distinction as wolves and dogs. Wolves represent independence and freedom that comes with a tougher path to survival, while dogs represent security and domestication, from the reliance of others.[6] I think it's a bit derogatory, but it delivers the point. While your closest friends and family will stick by you, they won't necessarily understand you.

The silver lining is that when you do find the group who "get" you, the affinity and bond can be much deeper. They're probably also applying some variation of *Asymmetric Principles*. But even those communities are too dynamic, and often are short-lived.

Outgrowing, Outgrown   A disheartening truth is that you will outgrow your peers, and your peers will outgrow you. That's not distinct from the rest of life. Growing apart is natural. But that process normally happens on a long enough time scale to make your transitions easier. The nature of *Asymmetric Principles* is that when you win, you win big and you win fast—that's the Super Upside. As a consequence of that, outgrowing or being outgrown can happen abruptly, which can be disorienting.

During my Y-Combinator batch in 2021, every company was a Slack message away. In smaller groups, we had formal catch-ups every week. Let's fast-forward a few years. Applying YC's past performance to the 377 companies in my batch, 67 (18%) will be worth more than $100 million, and 15 (4%) more than a billion.[7] Do you think founders of those billion-dollar companies will still be a Slack away? Most probably not. To be clear, this is usually not an issue of character, but one of structure. As I alluded to in Chapter 4 in the discussion of priorities, it's a resource issue. The nature of priorities, worries, and focus is vastly different between a founder tinkering to find product market fit and a founder building a team of a thousand generating hundreds of millions of dollars. You can be social and stay as friends, but it is fair to say that the two are no longer peers working through the same trenches. There are exceptions, of course, but those are certainly *despite* structural barriers, not because of them.

By the way, there is pain that comes both from being outgrown and outgrowing others. Each flavor of pain is different, but you'll feel pain one way or another applying *Asymmetric Principles*. To take a fantastical example, imagine you were part of a group of musicians who held song-writing sessions every weeknight. Let's say one of your personal digital singles pops off. You don't want to let this get to your head, and you want to continue your membership in this group. But then Max Martin—you know, only the greatest hitmaker of our time— calls you up and asks if you want to come by his studio to talk about a song that evening. You text your group chat apologetically and say you'll definitely be there for the next one. Then Ariana Grande DMs you saying she heard about your project with Max and invites you to fly over to her studio. You're going to go. It's Ariana. A few months down the line, your friends land their first big gig and ask you to perform with them at the local bar. "Of course," you say. You're going to make up for all your missed sessions. Then two days before the big day, BTS invites you to Korea to spend a month to cowrite their EP. Whatever you decide, you can see how over time, you will have outgrown the group, even if they remain your friends.

When you outgrow or are outgrown, it's best to accept and move on swiftly to minimize damage. In both cases, you'll face loneliness. At times, this will be accompanied by ugly emotions and misunderstandings. You'll be in a rupturing transitionary period between two peer groups—leaving one, but not yet settled in the other. When it inevitably happens, embrace it, and lean into that transition.

No One Cares. Just Get It Done   *Asymmetric Principles* requires you to make decision of consequence, which implies responsibility. By responsibility, I mean both backward- and forward-looking responsibility. Joel Feinberg articulates the conceptual difference between the two as such: backward-looking responsibility is accountability of past actions, and forward-looking responsibility focuses on duties regarding future actions. When a child spills a drink in a kindergarten classroom, backward-looking responsibility assigns blame to the child for spilling the drink, but the forward-looking responsibility assigns the duty of cleaning up the mess to the teacher.

What will happen in reality is that the teacher will also be assigned the backward-looking responsibility for not paying attention to the child in the first place. If it was unclear, the teacher is the metaphor for you—when bad things happen, you will be the person to blame. Very few will care about your circumstances when their own well-being is on the line. If you're not convinced, imagine being fired when your family's rent depends on your next paycheck. Consider your gut reaction. How much would the CEO's mental and physical health matter to you? Would it matter that the CEO spent weeks of sleepless nights to raise funding, before coming to the excruciatingly painful and humiliating decision of laying off the very people she convinced to join? Would you be curious about personal circumstances like a death of a family member or an accident that incapacitated the CEO? How much of it would matter even if you were curious enough to ask? Probably very little, if at all. As Mel Brooks once said "When I cut my finger, it's a tragedy. When you fall into an open sewer and die, it's comedy."[8] Many people will reduce you to the outcome you generate.

Stress of Uncertainty

In my view, realizing the Super Upside is a *matter of time* when you apply *Asymmetric Principles*. But putting up time as collateral indefinitely can feel like watching your fuel deplete mid-air without a landing spot in sight.

Certain Pain for Uncertain Reward   Unlike the Marshmallow Experiment that rewards a specific number of marshmallows at a specific time for delayed gratifications, *Asymmetric Principles* requires pain without certainty on the timing or the size of the reward. You could end up with a hundred marshmallows or lose the one marshmallow you have now. Oh, and you don't know when you'll find out.

The pain increases with larger swings. If my writing meant sacrificing a few Saturdays a month, my career swing meant taking a massive salary cut and spending most weekends in the office. The pain will feel very real, very quick. Observing counterfactuals only adds pressure. We all know *not* to do this, but it ends up happening anyway. In the course of starting my start-up, former colleagues and friends were hitting that seven-figure salary with impressive titles. Many were starting families and building wealth for a promising future. Others seemed to have perfected lifestyles of work and vacationing with their jobs. When you start taking asymmetric opportunities, waiting amidst uncertainty will be painful.

Loss of Control   Even if you've optimized every scenario to maximize your luck, you will not control the timing. The problem is that many of us have been trained to judge productivity as outcomes over *time*—to do more in as little time as possible. That works for predictable, scoped games like graduating college with a 4.0 GPA in two years instead of four or snagging an early promotion at a top consulting firm in 6 months instead of 12 months or finishing your PhD with five instead of two publications in major journals, and so on.

Asymmetric opportunities rarely have standard timelines or scope. Especially for people who've excelled in predictable systems, your Super Upside will take much longer than you might expect. I didn't get to decide that the first pre-seed investment would happen in meeting 8 or 158. I didn't decide if the first 10 scholarships were the winning ones or the next 100. You'll have the same issues in whatever asymmetric opportunity you take, from the number of auditions, applications, posts, coffee chats, or whatever else. You can't control the time, but it'll keep ticking. That can feel scary.

Predictable Point of Failure

Applying *Asymmetric Principles* exposes you to stressors at levels you wouldn't experience if you took a traditional path. And each of these stressors is deadly, increasing the risk of SPOF—the failure of you. Loneliness alone heightens the risk of premature death at levels on par with daily smoking according to the US Department of Health and Human Services. In several studies, they've found physical impacts, including 29% increased risk of heart disease, 32% increase in risk of stroke, and elevating risk of developing dementia by 50% in older adults.[9]

Stack on constant rejections, stress of uncertainty, and overworking, and you have a predictably bad outcome. I don't think I need to be a medical professional to be able to come to this conclusion. And though entirely predictable, many people have willfully ignored or truly been blindsided, which led to breaking points. Exploring this issue, I co-wrote a piece on mental health of founders with Carin-Isabel Knoop, the author of *Compassionate Management of Mental Health in the Modern Workplace* and the executive director at Harvard Business School. I'll share one study featured in the World Economic Forum where the author studied entrepreneurs, who compared to demographically matched comparison,[10] were:

- 10 times more likely to suffer from bipolar disorder
- 6 times more likely to suffer from ADHD
- 2 times more likely to suffer from depression and suicidal thoughts

Only after the point of permanent mental, physical, and social damage do many people finally acknowledge and address this. When left unaddressed, the damages come back in the most inopportune times with far more severity. The National Cancer Institute defines stress as "the body's response to physical, mental, or emotional pressure. Stress causes chemical changes in the body that can raise blood pressure, heart rate, and blood sugar levels."[11] There are real, physical stressors that impact your entire chemistry. The point of significance is that stressors are real, and often require far more than "positive thinking" or tricking your body into interpreting a stressor one way or another.

For clarity, not all stress is bad all the time. The issue at hand is persistent, prolonged stress. Chronic stressors that are poorly handled or left unaddressed are like grains of sand piling on top of you. It's tempting to ignore a single grain, until they become a heap that weighs you down, crushing you. To play the long game, it needs to be addressed.

As Muhammad Ali famously said, "It is not the mountains ahead to climb that wear you out; it's the pebble in your shoe."

Addressing Your SPOF

For *Asymmetric Principles* to be applied sustainably over a long period of time, predictable and reliable point of failure should be addressed. You are irreplaceable to you. Without you, no systems or returns matter. Being kind to yourself is how to address the SPOF, and eventually hit your Super Upside.

Showing that kindness to yourself manifests itself in many different ways, everywhere from optimal diet, sleeping habits, physical exercise, fulfillment, proper types of rest, social support systems, attitude, relationships, and hobbies, and can include taking care of your loved ones. Over time, everyone ends up building their own stack of what works for them. But there are far more informed researchers and scientists who can cover these topics with more detail and accuracy than I ever could in this book.

Instead, in the next chapter, I'll share one of the most predictable and damaging systemic failures that can occur while applying *Asymmetric Principles*. I'll follow that up with guidance on the unguided, taboo strategy: how to quit.

10

How to Quit

"Oops," said the man sitting next to me. Oops is not the word you want to hear when you're 5,000 ft up in the air. I looked at him in disbelief. With the siren of the Cessna 172 blaring, the nose of the plane dove toward the ground in a downward spiral. With my sweaty hands on the yolk, I muttered "PARE" under my breath.

During flight training, instructors can sometimes do nerve-racking things like turn off the engine mid-flight or pull the nose up until the wings exceed the critical angle of attack, which means no more lift—you know, the force that keeps the 1,800 pound hunk of metal in the air. That's called a stall. As the nose drops in a stall, the torque of the engine can cause the plane to yaw in one direction, causing the plane to spiral as it dives toward the ground. That's called a spin. What you don't want to do is follow your gut reaction and turn the yolk—the "steering wheel" of the plane—or aggressively pull the nose up. That'll aggravate the spin.

Today, pilots are taught to formulaically apply steps to regain control of the plane from this literal *downside* with a set of maneuvers called PARE: **P**ower to idle, push down the nose to adjust **A**ttitude to gain airspeed, slam our foot on the **R**udder to stabilize the plane, and then slowly pull up with the Elevators.[1] In fact, before procedures to recover from the spin were formally taught, some pilots ended up crashing. Pilots are taught these maneuvers precisely *ahead of* predictable downsides so we focus on executing the moves for recovery and ignore our instincts in disorienting situations. The spin equivalent for *Asymmetric Principles* is just as predictable as the worst-case scenario: giving up your agency.

The Worst-Case Scenario

"*I have control*" is a phrase to signal to my instructor that I will be making the calls during our flight. During urgent situations, I may say "*You have control*" for my instructor step in to guide us out of the danger zone. But the instructor can't be there forever if I want to be an independent pilot.

When I start flying solo—without the instructor—I legally become the Pilot in Command, or PIC, who has both *full agency* and *full responsibility* in the aircraft. For example, let's say Air Traffic Control (ATC) instructs me to descend to a certain altitude, without seeing another aircraft in the same vicinity. If I blindly follow instructions, and crash into the other aircraft, I'd be responsible. At the same time, if I refuse the ATC instructions and mess up the flight circuit of the airport, I'd also be responsible. Responsibility follows judgment. But imagine having your hands tied, with no authority to make that call and ultimately crashing into another aircraft. In my view, this is the worst-case scenario.

Giving Up Agency, While Bearing Full Responsibility

Parallels can be found in our lives. We all start with people who helped us navigate our lives, and took control in emergencies. But eventually we need to become the PIC of our own lives. When things get tough, it's tempting to look for an instructor to say "*you have control,*" or ATC to give you instructions. But at the end of the day, you are the one up in the air, at the controls, and you will bear the responsibility—not anyone giving you guidance from the comfort of their seats. Don't give up your agency.

Two Flavors

The pressures from the "ATCs" will increase as you apply *Asymmetric Principles* successfully. It will come from friends and family, co-workers, employees, financers, press, investors, customers, agencies, law firms, and so on. To make things worse, your biases and ego will come into play. If you're not careful, someone else will assume control, while you bear all responsibility—including the drop after the crash. Losing agency can come in two opposing pressures as we've seen throughout the book:

- Type I is prematurely ruling out a path for the wrong reason, often because the path is too hard or becoming demoralized, despite there being a real path to the Super Upside.
- Type II is ignoring the signals and sticking with a path for too long, often from ego and expectations of others. That error squanders your precious opportunity cost.

Neither one is conducive to properly applying your *Asymmetric Principles*. Of the two, I'll focus on the inability to quit—Type II—for a few reasons. First, there is considerable literature out there already documenting the benefits of grit, and the strategies that build grit. Even in this book, we've touched upon Duckworth's research on grit. In contrast, there is little guidance on when or even how to quit. Second, readers who put *Asymmetric Principles* into practice are the types who don't need cheerleaders to get through the hard times. You're probably not the type to quit just because someone tells you to.

On balance, I predict that the greater risk for those who apply *Asymmetric Principles* is sticking with the wrong thing for too long, rather than quitting too early.

Why I've Thought About Quitting

Quitting has pejorative connotations in the start-up and venture world. In fact, I've almost never seen anyone mention quitting with a positive light in that world. At best, it's tolerated. All success stories talk about resilience. Paul Graham in his essay *How Not to Die* noted, "If you can just avoid dying, you get rich. That sounds like a joke, but it's actually a pretty good description of what happens in a typical start-up."[2]

For clarity, quitting is different from failing. Failing is being *forced* to quit, and that's tolerated, and even celebrated with the start-up adage of "fail fast." In contrast, quitting implies voluntarily walking away. And like everyone else in the field, I never considered quitting as an option when I started my company. I was going to build a billion-dollar outcome or nothing at all. But that changed for me after a walk in Los Angeles.

A year into starting my start-up, I was crushing it. I had raised millions in the first six months of starting the company, launched the product, onboarded customers, and signed contracts with big players in the market. At the time, I was living in LA, and one of my investors was in town for an event. We met up at the Ritz Carlton and walked along Marina Del Rey. By the time our pace came to a rhythmic sync, he gave me a piece of advice, which in retrospect was kind advice. Here's a paraphrased version:

> "Daniel, you're doing a good job. I see your potential as a founder, and that's why I invested. But I want you to know it's okay to walk away if you feel like you've taken every shot and don't see a path forward. I'm not saying this because I think you'll fail. I'm saying this because I've seen founders who are trapped and stay for years—they were miserable. Many of those founders took a long time to recover."

When everything was going well, I didn't think much of this advice. But over time, I understood the kindness of his words, especially coming from an investor. For venture capitalists, a start-up is one of many in their portfolio. And investors often push founders to keep going. His advice was against his financial interest, at least in the short term. He reminded me there's more to life than a start-up, and I shouldn't allow others to make decisions that will crash my life.

Asymmetric Principles, especially when you see traction, can consume you. But remember that you are indisputably irreplaceable to at least one person, and that person is you. To avoid becoming stuck in the worst-case scenario, sometimes the right path to save yourself is to have a plan to quit.

Let me be clear. I'm not suggesting you quit whenever the going gets hard. I'm suggesting that you don't blindly write off quitting as an option and make a strategic decision with agency. Yes, quitting can be hard, but it can be the right strategy to sustainably build your life portfolio.

Why Quitting Is Hard

There is a technical, but unsatisfying reason why quitting is hard: because *not* quitting is easier. When you start seeing traction, all sorts of inertia come into play, from personal ego to social pressures to financial dependencies. The path of least resistance actually becomes slogging away even if you hate it. It takes an active decision against and courage to abandon your path. But that alone isn't why quitting might feel impossible.

Addicted to Potential

The Super Upside, as the words suggest, is pretty super. It's easy to get stuck in the land of potential. After all, it seems *plausible* that you *could* one day hit the Super Upside. Consider the following questions. Is it easier to see yourself as:

- A founder taking a shot at a billion-dollar company in a crappy studio in SF or a failed entrepreneur with no sense of financial responsibility?

- An aspiring actor working in the West Hollywood bar who'll be a star or a bygone talent with mediocre skills with no other options?
- A student preparing for medical or law school persevering for years to save lives or lacking self-awareness living in your parents' basement with no social life?
- A hopeless romantic with high standards for the perfect person or a constantly rejected single with no self-awareness?

I'm intentionally being harsh here, because the alternative—obsession with potential—is even worse. It is easy and tempting to hold on to what you could be. There are a number of reasons for why this occurs, including common phenomena such as sunk cost fallacies or loss aversion of killing your own potential and dream. You may be thinking, but isn't it true that the upside is within the realm of possibility? Sure, but so is pulling on the slot machine and hitting the jackpot.

In Chapter 6, I discussed the importance of precision in applying *Asymmetric Principles*, including its qualifiers. It's the details that prevent such pitfalls. Addiction to potential sacrifices the base case, and tolerates an unfloored downside without a clear path to the upside. Asymmetric upside isn't day dreaming. It's a clear, non-zero path to an uncapped upside. If your initial hypotheses were wrong, you need to either find alternative paths or write them off. Recall that the base case needs to take you where you need to go, and your downside should be predictable, tolerable, and floored. In every aspect, it falls outside the definition of *Asymmetric Principles*.

When applying *Asymmetric Principles* over a sustained period of time, it's important to stay mindful that initial scenario forecasts are not static. They will change with new information of experiments, passage of time, and the shift in the rest of your life portfolio. What was once considered a floored downside may become a bottomless pit, and your path to the Super Upside may be proven wrong. Understanding the sequence of events to signal that you're headed toward a downside is why I introduced downside optimizations in Chapter 3. Accurate assessment of downside scenarios with time-based milestones and pre-commitments to have an exit trigger needs to take place ahead of time. Making decisions as you live through the downside is extremely hard with your mental stress and brain space at its capacity.

Don't let yourself become blindly addicted to potential like a gambler for the "big win" to make up for your losses. Potential needs to actualize into reality eventually.

Growing Skin in the Game

In Chapter 7, I discussed the importance of building momentum. The flip side of having momentum is that stopping becomes harder, requiring active, and often painful, efforts to stop that momentum.

Suppose my start-up was stagnating. If my start-up had zero traction, zero customers, zero dollars, and zero team, shutting it down would be easy. But every time I advanced forward, it created a corresponding cost to quit: incorporating requires winding down the legal entity involving attorney fees, bank fees, and endless paperwork; fundraising requires returning capital that comes with physical friction like a dissolution contract and psychological friction like the fear of disappointing investors; and hiring requires laying off your early believers.

On top of that I'm required to take action that causes short-term pain, like cutting off a steady source of income and giving up on my dreams. Loss aversion is a powerful heuristic, and it turns out most people have more tolerance to keep on a familiar, predictably horrible path than to adopt a new one that may be better in the long run. These frictions increase the risk of maintaining your path even if there is no path forward. It doesn't stop with logistics either.

Identity Crisis In discussing reputation in Chapter 7, I mentioned *Asymmetric Principles* requires your own skin in the game. The more you grow, the more you stake. A side effect of investing your skin—reputation, capital, blood, sweat, tears—is that you start tying your personal identity to the outcomes of these opportunities. That's when the ego kicks in.

Everyone has an ego. It's a matter of degree and awareness. When ego gets in the way, quitting becomes exceptionally challenging. Not only is there a public admission of failure, but it also requires a painful blow to your identity. For example, if I were to shut down my own company, I'd feel as though I'm killing a part of my identity as a founder and replacing it with a far less flattering identity of a quitter. This line of reasoning follows most asymmetric opportunities. The more traction means more skin in the game, and often greater ties to your personal identity. It hurts to rip off your skin, but it's better than squandering your time.

Dysfunctional Beliefs About Quitting

Finally, quitting is hard because it is mischaracterized as a permanent, irreversible, suboptimal decision. We've almost been gaslighted into viewing quitting with almost every cliché of cognitive distortions that are out there (Table 10.1).

Table 10.1   Cognitive Distortions

Cognitive Distortion	Definition	Example
All-or-Nothing Thinking	Seeing things in black-and-white terms, without any middle ground.	"If I quit now, I'll quit forever."
Overgeneralization	Making broad conclusions from a single event.	"If I quit once, I'll always be a quitter."
Mind Reading	Assuming you know what others are thinking, especially negatively.	"People will think I quit because I didn't have what it takes."
Should Statements	Using unrealistic "should" or "must" statements.	"I should never give up."

Attractiveness of potential, growing skin in the game, and dysfunctional beliefs about quitting are a few reasons that make quitting a hard decision. But you should not allow these pressures to force your hand. Don't be fooled by the comfort and familiarity leading you toward a predictably catastrophic downside. You're in the pilot seat, and you will bear your consequences. Avoid the worst-case scenario of losing your agency.

During my own highs and lows of my start-up journey, I've thought deeply about quitting. A framework that helped me think through my own decision was looking past the pejorative connation of quitting for what it is. Quitting isn't an all-or-nothing deal. It's a tool like any other that can be used strategically.

Quitting as a Strategy

Let's not forget fundamentally what quitting is: it's an option that gives you the right, but not the obligation, to walk away. And options have value. If you think about it, options give you upside with little downside. When you leverage that value, quitting can be a powerful strategy for winners.

In the 2004 World Series of Poker Tournament of Champions, Annie Duke won the $2 million championship. She then went on to write one of the few books on quitting, *Quit: The Power of Knowing When to Walk Away*. In her talk at Wharton, she shared that a primary difference between elite players and amateurs is about how great you are at quitting. In her experience with Texas hold'em, for example, she found that pros fold 75–85% of the time before seeing any other cards, while amateurs play about 50% of the time.[3] That's before the betting even *starts*. Similar parallels exist, from plate discipline for batters in baseball to investors rejecting most companies in venture capital. They concentrate attention and resources on the few right things.

Figure 10.1   Four Types of Quitting

Broadening the Definition of Quitting

Quitting, when used well, can be powerful, especially in the context of iterative games like *Asymmetric Principles*. On a central theme of reversibility, I segmented the form of quitting to escape the worst-case scenario. Broadening the definition beyond a black-and-white view of quitting, I converged on four archetypes of quitting summarized in Figure 10.1.

Recalibrative Quitting Recalibrative quitting keeps your momentum with minor changes that are generally reversible and nonpermanent. It's broadly maintaining your direction while cutting off what doesn't work and focusing on what does. In my view, recalibrative quitting should almost be a permanent state of mind. An example of how this works in the world of start-ups would be *pivoting* (also echoed by Duke), which is a strategy that led to the success of many companies, including Instagram.

Instagram originally started out as Burbn, a location-based social app that allowed people to check in, collect points, and share photos. The founders observed that customers did not care about check-ins at all. Instead, customers used the photo-sharing feature with their friends. Once they realized that, the founders stripped out everything else in the app and focused on photo sharing. They continuously "quit" or pivoted through iterative experiments, eventually building the product as we know it today.[4] Founders were able to sniff out the right paths, and quit aspects of their direction to refocus on what works. These sorts of pivots are not isolated cases. Amazon, YouTube, Twitter, Slack, PayPal, and many other prominent companies are benefactors of recalibrative quitting,[5] which, by the way, isn't reserved just for start-ups, and is applicable to your life.

When I was building an AI tool to take long-form written content to short-form material, I had a chance to speak with many successful writers. Almost all of them had examples of recalibrative quitting from switching platforms, formats, and genres to find a path that works for them. The broad strokes of writing remained, but there was iterative quitting to refocus on what works as they grew.

Recalibrating, strictly speaking, is a form of quitting. But the broad direction remains the same, and it helps to reallocate resources on what works to continue to build your momentum.

Explorative Quitting At the end of the day, quitting crosses your mind because you don't have a 100% conviction on your path for one reason or another. Taking a break to try something with a natural course of reversion is *explorative quitting.*

Explorative quitting is common in traditional careers. In management consulting, many firms offer consultants options to explore their personal interests, from firm-sponsored MBAs, nonprofit rotations, and externships in industries. For more tenured staff, sabbaticals and leaves of absence are not uncommon. I've seen examples outside my direct industry, too. Most universities allow students to take gap years to explore different areas before returning and completing their degree. Law firms encourage lawyers to spend a year doing an LLM degree before returning to their firm. In tech, some engineers join a

temporary taskforce to work on internal projects outside their immediate teams. Each of these options has an embedded system that allows
you to return to your current position.

Explorative quitting is the most common form of quitting I rec-
ommend. It's a low-cost way that results in two great outcomes. If
you come back, you come back with greater conviction in your
choice and a broader perspective, network, and expertise that often
makes you more effective. If you don't come back, it was certainly
worth putting your position on hold to explore alternatives. At
worst, you quench your thirst of exploring with a more diverse
experience.

Elevative Quitting   Elevative quitting is stepping away to mend
gaps, whether in your values, skills, or character, and takes time and
effort to reverse. In the TV show *Suits*, Jessica Pearson has her mentee
Harvey Spector join a prosecutor's office for a few years before joining her corporate law firm. She saw gaps in courtroom experience in
corporate lawyers and wanted to mend that skill gap for her protégé,
Harvey. This is an example of elevative quitting.

In my life, venture investing is the one that comes to mind. My very
first exposure to VC was during an internship with the Business
Development Bank of Canada (BDC), a Canadian Crown Corporation that supports entrepreneurs in Canada. Splitting my time between
strategy and venture investment, I had a chance to evaluate companies at a local accelerator in Montreal. I felt like an idiot, and rightly
so, because I didn't know the first thing about what makes a
good start-up.

After BDC, I spent a few years in management consulting, working on
projects in product marketing, risk management, and procurement for
Fortune 500 companies. Those two years made me slightly better at
understanding how companies operate by the time I joined SoftBank.

Directly investing in companies and advising on boards at SoftBank developed my intuition and skills. Then I left once more.

Now, after a few years of working on my own start-up, I have a much better understanding of operations and inner working of start-ups. Collectively, iterative quitting made me an even better venture investor. That's not to say I'm committed to returning as an investor. In fact, each time I left, I didn't have formal mechanisms or obligations to return to investing. Yet, I found myself coming back to investing several times, each time with an elevated set of skills and experiences.

Games in life are far more iterative than you might think. Most types of quitting are reversible—though it takes some time and effort—and even elevative.

Committed Quitting   Committed quitting is the most radical version of quitting. Perhaps its extremity is why it has become the image that lives in people's mind. It is irreversible, high cost, and permanent, setting a high bar to pull the plug.

My contention is that quitting is rarely this extreme. The few that come to mind are time-bound opportunities such as dropping out of competitive physical sports that require peak athletic abilities; leaving pro-gaming that requires high reaction speeds; and missing the chance to spend time with a loved one in a particular stage of their life. Most decisions to quit are reversible, including leaving your job, switching your hobby, ending your side hustle, or even leaving relationships are rarely irreversible.

Broadening the definition of quitting can help maintain your agency by easing the friction to quit. Understanding the ranges of quitting can help make tactical decisions to apply *Asymmetric Principles*. For absolute clarity, I'm not advocating for quitting whenever something gets hard. In fact, you'll have to stick with *something* at *some point* in your life to see any success. It's a necessary but not sufficient condition of the Super Upside. That's where all the highly documented advice on grit, perseverance, and resilience comes in, to push through the hardships sustainably.

When to Consider Quitting

What I'm proposing is simple: not all resilience is good all the time, and not all quitting is bad all the time, especially if it's done in the right way. I don't think it's polemic to say there are good and bad reasons to quit.

You've Hit Your Triggers

As you live through your forecasted outcomes, there will come a time you hit the downside. In Chapter 3, I introduced the importance of time-based milestones as triggers and pre-commitments as exits planned ahead of time. That's the stuff that allowed you to floor the downside. When your downside scenario is triggered, follow the exit procedures you've placed ahead of time unless there is compelling new information. It's a bad idea to reason out other paths while your brain space is tapped out, your emotional response has been crushed, and your psychological state is in distress.

Think back to the beginning of this chapter, and imagine you're falling out of the sky. You don't want to be experimenting with new maneuvers while you're in a spiral dive. You will experience spatial disorientation with blurred sense of airspeed, direction, and altitude confusion in spiral dives. Depending on the angle, the G-force (force per unit mass) can triple in a *matter of seconds* with rapid increase in airspeed and crosses VNE (never exceed speed), causing the structural integrity of the plane to fail.[6] Relying on your judgment and coming up with a new plan while you're falling is a bad idea.

Keep Your Goalposts   A temptation during the downside is shifting goalposts. The problem with going a "little further" than your trigger is that you may be falling a lot faster than you think, especially if you've used leverage to scale. Be careful in toying around with choices with bottomless downsides.

In the past, I've seen companies in highly regulated spaces, skipping out on attorney review, to go a "little further" with their dwindling runway. While I don't know the details on its legality, the downside of a start-up can easily go from a tolerable floor to violating the law. That's the sort of judgment you want to avoid. In less dramatic cases, people wake up after decades have passed. It's the temptation of shifting goalposts by a palatable rate at a time—one more audition, one more month, one more customer, one more experiment, one more whatever—until one day you realize you've been stuck for too long. Trust your judgment of the past you, who reasoned this out. When you've hit your triggers, walk away.

No Path Forward, Despite Best Efforts

Burnout is a monster of a topic. There is considerable research on its causes and remedies that are highly nuanced. But the most common source of burnout I've observed in myself and others is less about what I put in and more about what I get out. It's the feeling of being stuck. Sam Altman echoes my sentiment in an interview with Lattice, a multibillion-dollar HR company backed by Y-Combinator: "In my own experience, what I found is that burnout actually comes from failing and things not working."[7]

In the context of *Asymmetric Principles*, burnout rarely happens when you are rapidly progressing toward your Super Upside. In contrast, burnout occurs when you don't see a viable path—opposite of a clear, non-zero path to the upside. That's when it falls outside the definition of *Asymmetric Principles*. Once you lose momentum, it's extremely hard to get it back. At times, it's better to start over from scratch than trying to build momentum for a path where you see no upside. But I'll caveat this with the words "despite best efforts."

Best Efforts to Minimize Regret   Best efforts is an important qualifier, because lacking it can become the biggest source of regret in your life. We've discussed the importance of considering both Type I and Type II errors in this book. If you're quitting with assurance of your best efforts, you can safely rule out the possibility of quitting too early. A good litmus I use is a hypothetical. If I could rewind time and do it over, would I go back? If there is apprehension because of the sheer work I've put in at the time, then I know I had given it my all, all things considered.

Your biggest regret will be if you've cheated yourself. It doesn't matter if you've fooled everyone into thinking you worked 100 hours a week. It doesn't matter if there are 100 reasons it wouldn't have worked. Only you will know deep down if you've truly given it your best efforts running your experiments. It's not the quitting that should be scary, but quitting without conviction. Don't cheat yourself.

Run Toward Rather Than Away

Iterative experimentation is at the heart of *Asymmetric Principles*. A second-order impact of testing your hypotheses is learning about the unknown unknowns. Experimenting can lead to serendipity and opportunities that are more attractive than your current set of forecast scenarios. Have awareness to recognize the insight, and that it can be an opportune time to quit.

Barring exceptional circumstances like abuse, it is better to quit moving toward something rather than running away from something. In my case, leaving SoftBank wasn't because I didn't like the job, but because I wanted to build a company. I wasn't running from but running toward. I've observed that most decisions made running away from something end with regret. That's another agency error, but on the opposite side of quitting.

Quit, Don't Quit, Decide

Since starting my company, the environment hasn't been ideal. Interest rate spikes killed our initial business model, AI replaced some of our capabilities, while tech valuations generally crashed. In 2022, I opened our Asia office, only to shut it down in 2023. My target timeline to create fair access to capital through my start-up—and on the way become a billion-dollar company—was, well, by 2024, when this book was submitted. The stark contrast between my ideal and reality pushed me to consider quitting.

Everything I've shared in this chapter is something I've thought about in my own journey of applying *Asymmetric Principles*. Ultimately, I've come to a decision to continue my start-up for right now. But it's not the outcome of the decision that matters per se, but that it was out of my own volition. When you apply *Asymmetric Principles*, there will be growing pressure to test your agency. Remember that you are one with full agency and full responsibility. Don't give in to the worst-case scenario. That includes, at times, taking a strategic decision to quit. Quitting is a notoriously under-guided path. I tried to cut through the negative connotations of quitting and reframe the idea of quitting as a strategy that comes in a spectrum from recalibrative to committed quitting. Strategically quitting can support you in your journey of finding your Super Upside.

Quit or don't quit. Whatever the outcome, it's easier to accept if it's happened under your judgment. Don't give up your agency for the benefit of convenience. You are the one who will live the consequences. Choose to be the Pilot in Command of your life. Make your own calls and own them. That includes how you'll take the *Asymmetric Principles* in your life.

11 | The Super Upside Hypothesis

My publisher and I had a minor dispute over the title for this book. Which word should come after The Super Upside? "*Factor*" or "*Hypothesis*"? It's semantics, but publishing experts pushed for the word *Factor,* which was assertive and attention-grabbing—both important to influence the split-second decision to buy the book. I deferred to their views—this was not the battle I needed to win.

That being said, I still think the word *hypothesis* encapsulates my mental model of *Asymmetric Principles* much more accurately. A working hypothesis implies both:

- High convictions from falsifiable experiments to date
- Flexibility to adapt the model based on new information in the future

Asymmetric Principles as I've presented to you in the book comes precisely from these two pillars. My hypothesis started with observations of principles that played out in industries and careers, and then I ran a series of iterative experiments in my own life. Each time, the principles would lead to either greater conviction or adjustments to the model. In contrast, *factor* could suggest a matter-of-fact manner, which runs contrary to the spirit of hypotheses and experimentation.

It's not dissimilar to Karl Popper's requirement of falsifiability in scientific methods.[1] Popper deems falsifiability—the possibility of being proven wrong—a demarcation criterion that separates science from non-science. "All swans are white" is a classic example. Your 1,000[th] time observing a white swan will create more conviction than your first, but it still leaves room for the possibility of a black swan. Over the years, I've built a strong enough conviction in this base model—enough to share with others in a rather permanent form of a book. But it's also true that *Asymmetric Principles* remains open, and I expect continued change over time. Change will happen not only from refinement of the framework itself, but also from the rapidly changing state of the world. The primary thesis of Chapter 4 was highlighting the risks of stagnation. Both drivers of change leave enough room for you to run your own experiments. *Asymmetric Principles* in the current state is the result of such changes.

In this final chapter, I'll share how *Asymmetric Principles* came into existence and discuss the core changes and limitations. And in the final page of the book, I'll conclude with a request to you, my readers.

Catalyst for Asymmetric Principles

Asymmetric Principles is heavily influenced by my personal experiences—reflections of my past, ongoing experiments in my life, and aspirations for my future. My personal belief is that everyone has the potential to reach their Super Upside. But only a few are positioned to achieve it.

My mission throughout my career, including my start-up, is about making that potential more accessible, just as others have generously done so for me, when I had little. Writing this book is an extension of this mission. Distilling learnings I've gathered across various contexts—as a pilot, consultant, investor, founder, and now a writer—I've formalized *Asymmetric Principles* into a framework I wish I'd had growing up, and the one I'll use to design my future.

Looking to the Past

Given the cards I've been dealt, I lucked out. The realized path I'm living, among many possible outcomes, is exceptionally good when I consider the *average* of possible outcomes of my background. "Given" in the first word of this paragraph is the key word here. When I immigrated to Canada with my family, I grew up on a farm in the province of Manitoba, in a small town called Otterburne that has fewer than 3,000 people.[2] Our income was well below the poverty threshold in Canada, and upon arriving in Canada I spoke very little English. Of course, there were many things going for me too – a loving family and a healthy body. But my hand was not exactly a pocket full of aces.

Under such circumstances, guidance for decision-making was far from refined. Often, I relied on imprecise systems and was overly influenced by intuitions I happened to hold at that time. I was gambling with life. The decisions we make in our early days may seem inconsequential, but they compound. What if I had taken that job at my friend's farm? What if I never met the friend who introduced me to a path as a pilot? What if I had taken the full ride in the local university instead of taking that risk to attend McGill? What if I spent all my time on part-time jobs instead of going all in on scholarship applications? Not to say the paths I didn't choose aren't formidable ones, but I cannot imagine finding something I enjoy as much as what I do today. And I'm grateful.

But gratitude is not mutually exclusive with desiring improvement. For both the good and the bad outcomes, I was at the mercy of systems I adopted to make those decisions—to reiterate Chapter 5, we all have systems, just a matter of which ones. *Asymmetric Principles* incorporates back tests that would have maximized my luck more consistently to a better set of outcomes. In other words, if I were to back test *Asymmetric Principles* as it stands to my past, would it reliably and consistently place me in the path of luck? The reason I share my past is not with the intent to invoke pity or aggrandize my efforts more than they deserve. The purpose is to share how I've thought about the design of *Asymmetric Principles* so *anyone* can adopt it, with or without a traditionally "elite" background. My story with its challenges of rural townships, immigration, and poverty hopefully serves as a testament to that. But of course, the utility of this framework for me comes for my future decisions.

Designing My Future

A recent study from Denmark suggested that every $10,000 in total family income leads to 2% higher likelihood to enter creative fields—artists, musicians, authors, actors. This trend holds quite linearly from an annual family income of $50,000 all the way up to $1,000,000, with the latter having 20 times higher probability to pursue creative careers.[3] These barriers are examples of risk restrictions at play.

The difference between risk restriction and risk aversion is the inability and unwillingness to take risks. Growing up, risk restriction was certainly the case. And my propensity to avoid all risk helped me survive, which developed into an instinct. But as I saw compounding benefits of *Asymmetric Principles*, these same instincts were getting in the way of my future, conflating risk aversion with restriction. *Asymmetric Principles* were designed with both in mind. As you saw in Chapter 3, the framework is flexible enough to allow for 15 minutes a day to an entire career to benefit even the most risk averse and risk restricted individuals to catch the Super Upsides without having to risk everything.

Decoupling Errors and Outcomes

Asymmetric Principles that I've shared in its form has changed significantly over the years through convictions and adjustments of hypotheses. Prescriptions and qualifiers are precise because I've lived through them with my own skin in the game over the last 15 years. Changes come from reflection of my own mistakes and learnings throughout the process. Without details, it's like loosely following a bread recipe, but skipping out on "small" details like yeast, and expecting to have a beautiful loaf of bread at the end of the process.

For my readers, I felt it would be worthwhile to share the change process, starting with how I've defined errors that led to these qualifiers. I define errors less as comparing realized outcomes of decisions after the fact, but more so as comparing ranges of outcomes at the point of decision-making. That is, the point of error occurs at decision-making, regardless of which outcomes are realized.

Well before Demo Day had started for YC, my seed round was oversubscribed, which means more written commitments to invest than we were willing to raise. Instead of increasing the round size, we declined investments beyond our original round target, which was a little shy of $3 million. Our rationale was to limit dilution (how much ownership we give away to investors) and work with investors we liked. We raised just enough to test our early hypotheses with a small buffer. Immediately after our raise, venture capital became scarce. When considering the realized outcome, it can look like the wrong decision. Taking the $5 million over $3 million seems like it would have been a better option based on outcomes. But I don't consider our decision to be an error. I made the call on a balance of probabilities, and had no idea the market crash would happen immediately after our raise.

Similarly, there are times where I had a better outcome from errors in my decision-making. In other words, I ask myself if I had a principled system to make a decision considering ranges of outcomes, rather than comparing two realized outcomes. I suppose one way of illustration is roulette. I wouldn't judge my decision on good or bad based on money I won from picking red. I'd evaluate my decision to even engage in a game that's stacked against me.

Changes with *Asymmetric Principles* will not end here. They will continue to improve over time through iterative experimentation and adaptation to the changing world. Perhaps there will be minor changes. Perhaps there will be major shifts. Just because the book is out, doesn't mean I don't have skin in the game. My experiments from Chapter 3 are ongoing, with many more to come as I continue to refine *Asymmetric Principles* so all of us can reach our Super Upside.

Closing Words to Readers

As much as I have conviction in *Asymmetric Principles* with deep personal ties and proven research, it is a framework that has its place for some things and not for others. Everything has trade-offs. No matter how refined it may become, there are things these principles are simply not designed to do.

What Asymmetric Principles Isn't

I deferred life questions back to the readers and refrained from normative statements. That's by design. *Asymmetric Principles* is not a framework to help you find the meaning of your life. It does not prescribe virtues or vices, nor does it tell you what you should want in life. That's for you to determine and act upon by getting to know yourself. *Asymmetric Principles* is a set of principles to maximize your chances of generating outsized returns while protecting yourself. While these principles can accelerate your path to learning about yourself and the world, the core of who you are and decisions you will make cannot be deferred to this framework. You need to answer those.

Not a Guide for Your Values   My mom choosing to serve our family is a quintessential example of where the framework doesn't apply. In Chapter 7, I introduced the idea of leverage to scale your initial upsides. The wisdom is to secure leverage for *your* outsized returns. My mom chose the opposite path. She focused on being a leverage *provider* for our family. It is because of her sacrifices that I have seen the little success I have today. I'm certain my sister, who's now a medical doctor, and my dad, who runs his own organization, share this sentiment. That is not to downplay the sacrifices my dad or my sister or even I made for our family. But insofar as personal careers and dreams are concerned, my mom sacrificed hers so we could have ours.

Asymmetric Principles would have advised a path directly contrary to her decision. Today, I'm doing the little I can to support her on her journey to become a writer. Perhaps your calling is to sell your possessions and serve the poor. Perhaps your values are with family while limiting work hours. Perhaps your lifelong dream is to open up your own café where you can hang out with your closest friends rather than scaling to a global franchise like a Starbucks or Blue Bottle. *Asymmetric Principles* is probably not the framework for those values or objectives.

Like everything else I've shared in the book, understand that every system has trade-offs: a time and place. *Asymmetric Principles* is a framework to help you realize your Super Upside while protecting you. It does not give prescription on values or way of life.

Not the Only Way to Play the Game Even if your objectives are the Super Upsides, different games reward different strategies. There are endless biographies of successful people in every category imaginable. Some put everything on the line, while others took calculated risks. Some mastered one thing in their entire career, while others engaged in multiple ventures. Some succeeded with contrarian truths, and others with accepted ones. Some are hedgehogs and others are foxes. *Asymmetric Principles* is one of these playbooks.

While I hold my position that *Asymmetric Principles* is the best framework to maximize your *chances* of hitting your Super Upside while protecting yourself, I'll point out that it does not guarantee success, and certainly not at a time of your choosing. For every one thing I've secured and shared with you in this book, there are several dozen that didn't work out. There is a folder on my computer with literally thousands of shots I've taken. Most of these have been rejected in silence. Life is not a simple problem, but a complex and chaotic one. What I will say, is that the graveyard of failures and rejections in my folder serves as evidence for my work and has become a source of confidence, rather than a source of failure or shame.

Am I ending the book with ambivalence? Absolutely not. Sharing the limitations of *Asymmetric Principles* does not detract my conviction that it is the best way to hit your Super Upside. An overarching theme throughout the entirety of the book was agency. I share the honest limits and boundaries to inform you to make your own call on how you make life decisions.

My Request to You

I thank you for taking your precious time to read to the end. In the final pages of the book, I want to make clear that I do not want to imply I'm among the greats or pretend I've "made it." I'm simply a peer, perhaps a few steps ahead of you or maybe a step or two behind you in our respective journeys. I'm right here with you figuring things out. *Asymmetric Principles* is my playbook for anyone to maximize luck of realizing the Super Upside, even if you are risk averse or even risk restricted. It's a solid start—a base model, so to speak—that will continue to be refined through iterative experiments. With that, I close with two requests.

Sharing my opinions in such intimate detail is unfamiliar to me, and even more so in the form of a book. Despite my best efforts, there will be imperfections. Please be kind and share your constructive feedback, so the best ideas remain, and new ones emerge in future iterations. My second request, if you are convinced of or intrigued by *Asymmetric Principles,* please share your experiments and outcomes with me at www.TheSuperUpside.com. Every one of you will be at different places in your journey from finding initial traction, scaling with leverage, and building your portfolios. And you'll be applying in new contexts I haven't yet explored. For me, the next few years will be a transitionary period from exploration to doubling down. By iterating with all of you, my hope is that we can converge on finding better frameworks faster through collective learning—a framework that will help others like you and me hit their own Super Upsides.

Upward and onward.

Notes

Chapter 1

1. Preqin. *Preqin Global Report 2023: Venture Capital*. London: Preqin Ltd., 2023. https://www.preqin.com/insights/global-reports/2023-venture-capital.
2. Gené Teare. "Global Funding 2023: How AI Drove a Surge in Investments." *Crunchbase News,* August 15, 2023. https://news.crunchbase.com/venture/global-funding-data-analysis-ai-eoy-2023/.
3. Paul Gompers, and Josh Lerner. *The Venture Capital Cycle* (Cambridge, MA: MIT Press, 1999).
4. Timeline: How Uber's Valuation Went from $60M in 2011 to a Rumored $50B This Month." *VentureBeat,* May 10, 2015. https://venturebeat.com/entrepreneur/timeline-how-ubers-valuation-went-from-60m-in-2011-to-a-rumored-50b-this-month/.
5. A. Eldridge. "Instagram." Encyclopedia Britannica, August 13, 2024. https://www.britannica.com/money/Instagram.
6. Bryce Elder. "Venture Capital Funds Are Mostly Just Wasting Their Time and Your Money." *Financial Times,* August 17, 2023. https://www.ft.com/content/2099d3c1-65ba-4c20-a50c-f730fd258f42.
7. David Coats. "Venture Capital: We're Still Not Normal." *VC by the Numbers,* July 13, 2023. https://correlationvc.com/insights/.

197

8. Kate Clark. "Sequoia Capital to Open New York Office, First U.S. Outpost Outside Silicon Valley—the Information." Information, July 27, 2022. https://www.theinformation.com/articles/sequoia-capital-to-open-new-york-office-first-u-s-outpost-outside-silicon-valley.

9. "Our History." n.d. Sequoia Capital US/Europe. https://www.sequoiacap.com/our-history/.

10. Eric Pfanner. "Softbank's Alibaba Alchemy: How to Turn $20 Million Into . . ." *Wall Street Journal*. September 19, 2014. https://www.wsj.com/articles/BL-DGB-37805.

11. Josh Constine. "21 Years and $4 Million Later, I Finally Have a Hit." *TechCrunch,* June 26, 2013. https://techcrunch.com/2013/06/26/21-years-4-million-dollars/.

12. Adobe. "Adobe to Acquire Figma." *Adobe Newsroom,* September 15, 2022. https://news.adobe.com/news/news-details/2022/Adobe-to-Acquire-Figma/default.aspx.

13. Iain Martin. "Danny Rimer Makes Midas in Europe with Figma-Adobe Deal." *Forbes,* December 8, 2022. https://www.forbes.com/sites/iainmartin/2022/12/08/danny-rimer-midas-europe-index-figma-adobe/.

14. Microsoft. "Microsoft to Acquire LinkedIn." *Microsoft News Center,* June 13, 2016. https://news.microsoft.com/2016/06/13/microsoft-to-acquire-linkedin/.

15. Microsoft. "Microsoft Acquires GitHub." *Microsoft News Center,* October 26, 2018. https://news.microsoft.com/announcement/microsoft-acquires-github/.

16. Amazon.com, Inc. "2015 Letter to Shareholders." April 2016. https://ir.aboutamazon.com/annual-reports-proxies-and-shareholder-letters/default.aspx.

17. Bill Ackman (@BillAckman). "My best and favorite investments come from a deep understanding of the importance of asymmetry, that is, by understanding the potential risk and reward, and making sure that the reward overwhelming compensates for the risk.

I have made some great asymmetric investments at Pershing Square, and also personally in start ups. My first venture capital investment returned 1,650 times my initial investment, and I am fortunate to have had a number of other great ones, but none quite so good as the first." X (formerly Twitter), January 13, 2024. https:// x.com/BillAckman/status/1746381227798487424?lang=en.

18. Nassim Nicholas Taleb. *Fooled by Randomness: The Hidden Role of Chance in Life and in the Markets*. 2nd ed. (New York: Random House, 2005), 103.

19. Sam Altman (@sama). "The best work you ever do is what matters, not the time you worked on alchemy. Optimize for being spectacularly right some of the time, and low-stakes wrong a lot of the time." X (formerly Twitter), January 6, 2020. https:// twitter.com/sama/status/1214274041176920064.

Chapter 2

1. Douglas Busvine. "AUTO1 Shares Go into Top Gear in Frankfurt Debut." *Reuters*, February 4, 2021. https://www.reuters.com/ article/business/auto1-shares-go-into-top-gear-in-frankfurt-debut- idUSL8N2KA2LE/.

2. Arjun Reddy. "Uber Is Going Public at a $75.5 Billion Valuation. Here's How That Stacks Up." *Entrepreneur*, May 10, 2019. https:// www.entrepreneur.com/business-news/uber-is-going-public-at- a-755-billion-valuation-heres/333583.

3. First Round Capital. "There's a .00006% Chance of Building a Billion Dollar Company: How This Man Did It." *First Round Review*. March 6, 2024. https://review.firstround.com/theres-a- 00006-chance-of-building-a-billion-dollar-company-how-this- man-did-it/.

4. Monica Mercuri. "BTS' Jung Kook Breaks Spotify's 1 Billion Streams Record." *Forbes*, November 6, 2023. https://www.forbes .com/sites/monicamercuri/2023/10/31/bts-jung-kook-breaks- massive-streaming-record-making-spotify-history/.

5. Charlie Harding. "Billie Eilish, the Neo-Goth, Chart-Topping Teenage Pop Star, Explained." *Vox*, August 19, 2019. https://www.vox.com/culture/2019/4/18/18412282/who-is-billie-eilish-explained-coachella-2019.

6. Billie Eilish. "Billie Eilish—Ocean Eyes (Official Music Video)," March 24, 2016. https://www.youtube.com/watch?v=viimfQi_pUw.

7. The Decision Lab. "Precommitment—the Decision Lab," n.d. https://thedecisionlab.com/reference-guide/psychology/precommitment.

8. Jon Elster. "Ulysses and the Sirens: A Theory of Imperfect Rationality." *Social Science Information* 16, no. 5 (August 1, 1977): 469–526. https://doi.org/10.1177/053901847701600501.

Chapter 3

1. Riley De León. "How SoftBank and Its $100 Billion Vision Fund Has Become a Global Start-up Machine." CNBC, May 20, 2019. https://www.cnbc.com/2019/05/17/softbanks-100-billion-vision-fund-reshapes-world-of-venture-capital.html.

2. Bernhard Schroeder. "How to Avoid Being in the 90% of Entrepreneurial Startups Who Fail. Six Insights on How to Find Real Problems." *Forbes*, June 15, 2023. https://www.forbes.com/sites/bernhardschroeder/2023/06/15/how-to-avoid-being-in-the-90-of-entrepreneurial-startups-who-fail-six-insights-on-how-to-find-real-problems/.

3. Britannica, The Editors of Encyclopaedia. "Apollo 13." *Encyclopedia* Britannica, July 22, 2024. https://www.britannica.com/topic/Apollo-13-mission.

4. Jon Russell. "SoftBank's Massive Vision Fund Raises $93 Billion in Its First Close." *TechCrunch*, May 21, 2017. https://techcrunch.com/2017/05/20/softbank-vision-fund-first-close/.

5. Marisa Dellatto. "Justin Bieber Sells Music Rights for Over $200 Million to Hipgnosis Songs Capital." *Forbes*, January 24, 2023. https://www.forbes.com/sites/marisadellatto/2023/01/24/justin-bieber-sells-music-rights-for-over-200-million-to-hipgnosis-songs-capital/.

6. Olivia Singh. "Talent Manager Scooter Braun's Biggest Clients, from Justin Bieber to Ariana Grande." Business Insider, August 26, 2023. https://www.businessinsider.com/list-of-artists-that-scooter-braun-manages-2019-7#rising-country-music-star-callista-clark-is-also-part-of-the-sb-projects-roster-24.

7. CBC. "How Justin Bieber Proved That YouTube Can Produce Pop Stars," June 7, 2019. https://www.cbc.ca/music/how-justin-bieber-proved-that-youtube-can-produce-pop-stars-1.5163197.

8. John Maxwell Company. "From Making Cabinets to Making Millions—John Maxwell." John Maxwell, April 24, 2011. https://www.johnmaxwell.com/blog/from-making-cabinets-to-making-millions/.

Chapter 4

1. Team Coco. "Conan O'Brien's 2011 Dartmouth College Commencement Address | CONAN on TBS." June 12, 2011. https://www.youtube.com/watch?v=KmDYXaaT9sA.

2. Alexander Hermann, Harvard Joint Center for Housing Studies, Housing Perspectives. "Home Price to Income Ratio Reaches Record High." January 22, 2024. https://www.jchs.harvard.edu/blog/home-price-income-ratio-reaches-record-high-0.

3. US Census Bureau. "Income in the United States: 2022." Census.gov, September 12, 2023. https://www.census.gov/library/publications/2023/demo/p60-279.html.

4. Jessica Dickler. "62% of Americans Are Still Living Paycheck to Paycheck, Making It 'The Main Financial Lifestyle,' Report Finds." CNBC, October 31, 2023. https://www.cnbc.com/2023/10/31/62percent-of-americans-still-live-paycheck-to-paycheck-amid-inflation.html.

5. The Economist. "Japan and South Korea Are Struggling with Old-Age Poverty." *The Economist,* May 2, 2024. https://www.economist.com/asia/2024/05/02/japan-and-south-korea-are-struggling-with-old-age-poverty.

6. "Korean Crisis and Recovery." September 12, 2002. https://www.imf.org/external/pubs/nft/seminar/2002/korean/.

7. Byeong-Hwa Ryu. "Korea's NPS Sees Record Assets, Profit on Double-Digit Return." *KED Global*, January 15, 2024. https://www.kedglobal.com/pension-funds/newsView/ked20240 1020016.

8. Kang Koo Lee, Seung-Ryong Shin, and KDI. "Korea's National Pension: Structural Reform Measures." Report. *KDI FOCUS*. Vol. 129, 2024.

9. Julia Belluz, and Sarah Frostenson. "Why South Koreans Now Live Longer Than Americans." *Vox*, February 9, 2018. https://www.vox.com/2017/2/21/14684686/winter-olympics-pyeong chang-2018-health-life-expectancy.

10. Gateway to Global Aging Data (2024). Gateway Policy Explorer: Republic of Korea, Public Own Old-Age Benefit Plan Details, 1992-2022, Version: 1.1 (August 2023), University of Southern California, Los Angeles. https://doi.org/10.25553/gpe.ret.oa.kor.

11. Datadot. "Republic of Korea," n.d. https://data.who.int/countries/410.

12. Justin McCurry. "South Korea's Fertility Rate Sinks to Record Low Despite $270bn in Incentives." *The Guardian*, February 29, 2024. https://www.theguardian.com/world/2024/feb/28/south-korea-fertility-rate-2023-fall-record-low-incentives.

13. Jung-Hwan Hwang. "NPS Likely to Give Full Rights on Asset Management to Experts." *KED Global*, August 25, 2023. https://www.kedglobal.com/pension-funds/newsView/ked202308 250017.

14. Matthew Loh. "Elon Musk Says Laying Off 80% of Twitter's Staff Was 'Painful' and 'One of the Hardest Things' He's Had to Do as the Platform's Boss." *Business Insider*, April 12, 2023. https://www.businessinsider.com/elon-musk-laying-off-twitter-was-painful-bbc-spaces-interview-2023-4.

15. Layoffs.fyi. "Layoffs.fyi—Tech Layoff Tracker and Startup Layoff Lists." February 23, 2024. https://layoffs.fyi/.

Chapter 5

1. Bernhard Schroeder. "Entrepreneurs and Small Business Owners: Steve Job's Advice on Saying No More Often to Achieve Your Goals." *Forbes*, November 8, 2022. https://www.forbes.com/sites/bernhardschroeder/2022/10/31/entrepreneurs-and-small-business-owners-steve-jobs-advice-on-saying-no-more-often-to-achieve-your-goals/.

2. Amanda Reill. "A Simple Way to Make Better Decisions." *Harvard Business Review*, December 6, 2023. https://hbr.org/2023/12/a-simple-way-to-make-better-decisions.

3. James Clear. *Atomic Habits: An Easy & Proven Way to Build Good Habits & Break Bad Ones*, 2018. https://catalog.umj.ac.id/index.php?p=show_detail&id=62390.

4. "PSYC 110 - Lecture 17—a Person in the World of People: Self and Other, Part II; Some Mysteries: Sleep, Dreams, and Laughter | Open Yale Courses," n.d. https://oyc.yale.edu/psychology/psyc-110/lecture-17.

5. Herbert A. Simon. "Rational Choice and the Structure of the Environment." *Psychological Review* 63, no. 2 (1956): 129–138.

6. David Landy, Noah Silbert, and Aleah Goldin. "Estimating Large Numbers." *Cognitive Science* 37, no. 5 (2013): 775–99, 10.1111/cogs.12028.

7. Francis Galton. *Inquiries into Human Faculty and Its Development* (London: Macmillan, 1883).

8. Jean Piaget. *The Child's Conception of Number* (London: Routledge, 1952).

9. Stanislas Dehaene. *The Number Sense: How the Mind Creates Mathematics*, rev. ed. (Oxford: Oxford University Press, 2011).

10. Stanislas Dehaene, Véronique Izard, Elizabeth Spelke, and Pierre Pica. "Log or Linear? Distinct Intuitions of the Number Scale in Western and Amazonian Indigene Cultures." *Science (New York, N.Y.)*, 320, no. 5880 (2008), 1217–1220. 10.1126/science.1156540.

11. Stanley Milgram. *Obedience to Authority: An Experimental View* (New York: Harper & Row, 1974).

12. Philip G. Zimbardo. *The Lucifer Effect: Understanding How Good People Turn Evil* (New York: Random House, 2007).

13. Nir Eyal. *Indistractable: How to Control Your Attention and Choose Your Life* (London: Bloomsbury Publishing, 2019).

14. Paul Bloom. "Can Prejudice Ever Be a Good Thing?" n.d., https://www.ted.com/talks/paul_bloom_can_prejudice_ever_be_a_good_thing?subtitle=en.

15. World Economic Forum. "What We Learned About Effective Decision Making from Nobel Laureate Daniel Kahneman," April 2, 2024. https://www.weforum.org/agenda/2024/03/what-we-learned-from-nobel-winner-daniel-kahneman.

16. Daniel Kahneman, *Thinking, Fast and Slow* (London: Penguin UK, 2011).

17. Robert S. Siegler and Julie L. Booth. "Development of Numerical Estimation in Young Children." *Child Development* 75, no. 2 (2004): 428–444.

18. Rebecca Baldridge. "Top 10 U.S. Hedge Funds of August 2024." *Forbes Advisor*, April 8, 2024. https://www.forbes.com/advisor/investing/top-hedge-funds/.

19. Ray Dalio. *Principles: Life and Work* (New York: Simon & Schuster, 2017).

Chapter 6

1. Serguei Netessine. "What Covid Teaches Us About Innovating Fast," *Financial Times*, May 9, 2021, https://www.ft.com/content/4c69a6e5-8bb3-4be0-9674-11f2c21976b7.

2. Nassim Nicholas Taleb. *Skin in the Game: Hidden Asymmetries in Daily Life* (New York: Random House, 2018).

3. "Born in the Trades, Built for the Trades: Chapter 1. Introduction | Contractor Playbook." ServiceTitan, n.d. https://www.servicetitan.com/field-service-management/leadership.

4. Alex Konrad. "ServiceTitan, Software Provider for Tradespeople, Reaches $8.3 Billion Valuation," *Forbes*, March 26, 2021,

https://www.forbes.com/sites/alexkonrad/2021/03/26/servicetitan-software-provider-for-tradespeople-reaches-85-billion-valuation/.

5. Balaji S. Srinivasan. *Lecture 5: Market Research, Wireframing, and Design* (Startup Engineering Class, Stanford University, 2013), accessed August 28, 2024. https://spark-public.s3.amazonaws.com/startup/lecture_slides/lecture5-market-wireframing-design.pdf.

6. Joanne Chen. "American Dreamers: Andy Fang, Co-Founder of DoorDash, on How a Class Project Turned into a Massive Food-Delivery Service in America." *Forbes*, August 3, 2022. https://www.forbes.com/sites/joannechen/2022/07/31/american-dreamers-andy-fang-co-founder--cto-of-doordash-on-turning-a-school-project-into-feeding-america/.

7. Derek Saul. "Uber Sets Profit Record as Lyft and DoorDash Keep Losing Money." *Forbes*, February 20, 2024. https://www.forbes.com/sites/dereksaul/2024/02/07/uber-sets-profit-record-as-lyft-and-doordash-keep-losing-money/.

8. "Confronting Slavery in the Classical World | Emory | Michael C. Carlos Museum." n.d. https://carlos.emory.edu/exhibition/confronting-slavery-classical-world.

9. Rob Fitzpatrick. *The Mom Test: How to Talk to Customers and Learn If Your Business Is a Good Idea When Everyone Is Lying to You* (CreateSpace Independent Publishing Platform, 2013).

10. "'The Distractor' by James Bridle." n.d. https://digilab.kunsthaus.ch/en/digital-art/the-distractor-by-james-bridle.

11. "James Bridle / the Distractor." n.d. https://jamesbridle.com/works/the-distractor.

12. Tom Wujec. "Build a Tower, Build a Team" n.d. https://www.ted.com/talks/tom_wujec_build_a_tower_build_a_team?subtitle=en.

13. Scott D. Anthony. "Innovation Leadership Lessons from the Marshmallow Challenge." *Harvard Business Review*, December 6, 2017, https://hbr.org/2014/12/innovation-leadership-lessons-from-the-marshmallow-challenge.

14. Tom Wujec. "Build a Tower, Build a Team." n.d. https://www.ted .com/talks/tom_wujec_build_a_tower_build_a_team?subtitle=en.

15. Paul Graham. "Do Things That Don't Scale." *Paul Graham Essays*, July 2013. https://paulgraham.com/ds.html.

Chapter 7

1. Adam Grant. *Hidden Potential: The Science of Achieving Greater Things* (Random House, 2023), 108.

2. Air Cadet League of Canada. "History—Air Cadet League of Canada," July 7, 2014. https://aircadetleague.com/about-us/history/.

3. "MANITOBA AIR CADET PROGRAM/the Air Cadet Story - Part 4." n.d. https://web.archive.org/web/20160107104109/ http://www.aircadetleaguemb.ca/story4.html.

4. Brent Gleeson. "9 Navy SEAL Sayings That Will Improve Your Organization's Ability to Lead Change." *Forbes*. December 10, 2021, https://www.forbes.com/sites/brentgleeson/2018/07/ 23/9-navy-seal-sayings-that-will-improve-your-organizations-ability-to-lead-change/.

5. Eric Jorgenson. "FIND a POSITION OF LEVERAGE—Almanack of Naval Ravikant." Almanack of Naval Ravikant, September 15, 2020. https://www.navalmanack.com/almanack-of-naval-ravikant/find-a-position-of-leverage.

6. "Bob Sternfels Re-elected Global Managing Partner of McKinsey & Company." McKinsey & Company, February 1, 2024. https://www.mckinsey.com/about-us/new-at-mckinsey-blog/ bob-sternfels-re-elected-global-managing-partner-of-mckinsey-and-company.

7. Will Kenton. "The Big 4 Accounting Firms: An Overview." Investopedia, May 31, 2024. https://www.investopedia.com/ terms/b/bigfour.asp.

8. Principles by Ray Dalio. "How the Economic Machine Works by Ray Dalio." September 22, 2013. https://www.youtube.com/ watch?v=PHe0bXAIuk0.

9. Reuters. "Softbank Just Shocked Its Critics by Landing the Biggest Profit in the History of a Japanese Company." CNBC, May 12, 2021. https://www.cnbc.com/2021/05/12/softbank-joins-top-corporate-earners-with-its-37-billion-vision-fund-profit.html.

10. "BlackRock Reports Full Year 2023 Diluted EPS of $36.51, or $37.77." BlackRock, n.d. https://www.blackrock.com/corporate/newsroom/press-releases/article/corporate-one/press-releases/blackrock-reports-full-Year-2023-diluted.

11. Bob Pisani. "BlackRock's ETF Business Just Keeps Growing, but the Search for Revenue Goes On." CNBC, July 17, 2024. https://www.cnbc.com/2024/07/15/blackrocks-etf-business-just-keeps-growing-but-the-search-for-revenue-goes-on.html.

12. Drew Hansen. "This LinkedIn Data Scientist Suggests 10 Ways to Excel in Her Field." *Forbes*, January 2, 2017. https://www.forbes.com/sites/drewhansen/2016/11/29/data-scientist-habits/.

Chapter 8

1. The Fraser Institute. "There Are No Solutions to Canada's Housing Crisis—only Trade-offs." Fraser Institute, April 24, 2024. https://www.fraserinstitute.org/article/there-are-no-solutions-to-canadas-housing-crisis-only-trade-offs.

2. Matt Haig. *The Midnight Library* (Wheeler Publishing, Incorporated, 2021).

3. Isaiah Berlin. *The Hedgehog and the Fox: An Essay on Tolstoy's View of History—2nd ed.* (Princeton University Press, 2013), 2.

4. James Charles Collins, *Good to Great: Why Some Companies Make the Leap—and Others Don't* (Random House, 2001). 90–119.

5. "Altos Ventures." n.d. https://altos.vc/blog/foxes-and-hedgehogs/.

6. "Library of Congress Aesop Fables." n.d. https://read.gov/aesop/120.html.

7. The Diary of a CEO. "Jimmy Carr: 'There's a Crisis Going on With Men!'" April 15, 2024. https://www.youtube.com/watch?v=uHLAazKUU68.

8. Frans Johansson. *Medici Effect: What You Can Learn from Elephants and Epidemics* (Harvard Business Press, 2006).

9. Tae Kim. "Buffett, Quoting Partner Munger, Says There Are Three Ways to Go Broke: 'Liquor, Ladies and Leverage.'" CNBC, February 26, 2018. https://www.cnbc.com/2018/02/26/buffett-says-out-of-the-three-ways-to-go-broke-liquor-ladies-and-leverage-leverage-is-the-worst.html.

10. Britney Nguyen. "WeWork's Rise to $47 Billion—And Fall to Bankruptcy: A Timeline." *Forbes*, November 9, 2023. https://www.forbes.com/sites/britneynguyen/2023/11/07/weworks-rise-to-47-billion-and-fall-to-bankruptcy-a-timeline/.

11. Alex Wilhelm and Mary Ann Azevedo. "Fast Shuts Doors After Slow Growth, High Burn Precluded Fundraising Options." *TechCrunch*, April 6, 2022. https://techcrunch.com/2022/04/05/fast-shuts-doors-after-slow-growth-high-burn-precluded-fundraising-options/.

12. Johanna Englundh. "Credit Suisse's Demise: A Timeline of Scandal and Failures." Morningstar CA, March 21, 2023. https://www.morningstar.ca/ca/news/233244/credit-suisses-demise-a-timeline-of-scandal-and-failures.aspx.

13. "Law of the Instrument—the Decision Lab." The Decision Lab, n.d. https://thedecisionlab.com/biases/law-of-the-instrument.

14. Bernice T. Eiduson. *Scientists: Their Psychological World* (Basic Books, 1962).

15. Tim Harford. "A Powerful Way to Unleash Your Natural Creativity." n.d. https://www.ted.com/talks/tim_harford_a_powerful_way_to_unleash_your_natural_creativity/transcript?subtitle=en.

16. Stacy Daugherty. "John Coltrane Illustrates the Mathematics of Jazz | American Jazz Music Society." American Jazz Music Society, January 3, 2021. https://www.americanjazzmusicsociety.com/blog/john-coltrane-draws.

17. Elise Cutts. "Secret Mathematical Patterns Revealed in Bach's Music." *Scientific American*, February 20, 2024. https://www.scientificamerican.com/article/secret-mathematical-patterns-revealed-in-bachs-music/.

18. Iannis Xenakis, and Sharon E. Kanach. "Formalized Music: Thought and Mathematics in Composition." *Choice Reviews Online* 30, no. 01 (1992): 30–0194. 10.5860/choice.30-0194.

19. "Kantar BrandZ MostValuable Global Brands 2024." n.d. https://www.kantar.com/campaigns/brandz/global.

20. Dani Di Placido. "MrBeast Just Conquered YouTube—What's Next?" *Forbes*, June 5, 2024. https://www.forbes.com/sites/danidiplacido/2024/06/04/mrbeast-officially-conquered-youtube---now-what/.

21. Anandi Mani et al. "Poverty Impedes Cognitive Function." *Science* 341, no. 6149 (August 30, 2013): 976–980, 10.1126/science.1238041.

22. "Bloomberg." n.d. June 1, 2023. https://www.bloomberg.com/company/press/generative-ai-to-become-a-1-3-trillion-market-by-2032-research-finds/.

23. "Bloomberg." n.d.. February 22, 2024. https://www.bloomberg.com/professional/insights/sustainable-finance/esg-aum-set-to-top-40-trillion-by-2030-anchor-capital-markets/.

24. Naval (@naval). "Every single tweet costs nothing and has the potential to reach the entire world. It's the best lottery ever made." X (formerly Twitter), April 20, 2020. https://x.com/naval/status/1252394751837392898.

25. "Shopify Announces Fourth-Quarter and Full-Year 2023 Financial Results." Shopify, n.d. https://www.shopify.com/news/shopify-announces-fourth-quarter-and-full-year-2023-financial-results.

26. Melissa Dittmann. "Standing Tall Pays off, Study Finds." https://www.apa.org, n.d. https://www.apa.org/monitor/julaug04/standing.

27. Paul C. Quinn et al. "Preference for Attractive Faces in Human Infants Extends Beyond Conspecifics." *Developmental Science* 11, no. 1 (2007): 76–83, /10.1111/j.1467-7687.2007.00647.x.

28. Agnieszka Sorokowska, Piotr Sorokowski, and Jan Havlíček. "Body Odor Based Personality Judgments: The Effect of Fragranced Cosmetics." *Frontiers in Psychology* 7 (April 18, 2016), 10.3389/fpsyg.2016.00530.

Chapter 9

1. Sarah Chea. "Kakao Unveils First Independent Data Center After Five-Day Outage in 2022." June 12, 2024. https://koreajoon gangdaily.joins.com/news/2024-06-12/business/tech/Kakao-unveils-first-independent-data-center-after-fiveday-outage-in-2022/2067185.

2. "Kakao." *Q2 2024 Earnings Presentation*, May, 2024, kakaocorp .com. https://www.kakaocorp.com/ir/referenceRoom/earn ingsAnnouncement?lang=en.

3. "카카오, '데이터센터 화재' 서비스 장애 피해 보상 마무리." KBS 뉴스, June 30, 2023. https://news.kbs.co.kr/news/pc/view/ view.do?ncd=7712575.

4. "Summary of the Amazon EC2 and Amazon RDS Service Disruption in the US East Region." Amazon Web Services, Inc., n.d. https://aws.amazon.com/message/65648/.

5. Leena Rao. "Amazon's Market Cap Passes $100 Billion." *TechCrunch*, May 5, 2024. https://techcrunch.com/2011/07/27/ amazons-market-cap-passes-100-billion/.

6. Nassim Nicholas Taleb. *Skin in the Game: Hidden Asymmetries in Daily Life* (New York: Random House, 2018).

7. Jack Kelly. "Y Combinator Startups That Could Be the Next Tech Unicorns." *Forbes*, June 4, 2024. https://www.forbes.com/sites/ jackkelly/2024/06/04/y-combinator-startups-that-could-be-the-next-tech-unicorns/.

8. New Yorker. "The Demise of Physical Comedy." *The New Yorker*, June 28, 2013, https://www.newyorker.com/culture/richard-brody/the-demise-of-physical-comedy.

9. Office of the Assistant Secretary for Health (OASH). "New Surgeon General Advisory Raises Alarm About the Devastating

Impact of the Epidemic of Loneliness and Isolation in the United States." *HHS.Gov*, May 3, 2023. https://www.hhs.gov/about/news/2023/05/03/new-surgeon-general-advisory-raises-alarm-about-devastating-impact-epidemic-loneliness-isolation-united-states.html.

10. "There Is a Mental Health Crisis in Entrepreneurship. Here's How to Tackle It." World Economic Forum, February 8, 2020. https://www.weforum.org/agenda/2019/03/how-to-tackle-the-mental-health-crisis-in-entrepreneurship/.

11. "NCI Dictionary of Cancer Terms." Cancer.gov, n.d. https://www.cancer.gov/publications/dictionaries/cancer-terms/def/stress.

Chapter 10

1. Joseph Bourque. "The Spin Debate." *Smithsonian Magazine*, November 15, 2013. https://www.smithsonianmag.com/air-space-magazine/the-spin-debate-3571421/#:~:text=PARE%20is%20an%20acronym%20developed,un%2Dstall%20the%20wing).

2. Paul Graham. "How Not to Die." *Paul Graham Essays*, August 2007. https://paulgraham.com/die.html.

3. Wharton School. "Annie Duke Interview W/ Adam Grant on Knowing When to Quit – Authors@Wharton Event." November 30, 2022. https://www.youtube.com/watch?v=zwZdYgCEN70.

4. Mg Siegler. "A Pivotal Pivot." *TechCrunch*, May 5, 2024. https://techcrunch.com/2010/11/08/instagram-a-pivotal-pivot/.

5. Prathima Pinnamaneni. "From Instagram to Slack: 9 Successful Startup Pivots." CB Insights Research, June 26, 2020. https://www.cbinsights.com/research/startup-pivot-success-stories/.

6. "Proficiency: Recovery Procedures." Aircraft Owners and Pilots Association (AOPA), n.d. https://www.aopa.org/news-and-media/all-news/2020/november/pilot/proficiency-recovery-procedures.

7. Lattice. "Sam Altman on How to Make an Impact on the World." October 18, 2016. https://www.youtube.com/watch?v=KhLh87MdbhI.

Chapter 11

1. Karl Popper, *The Logic of Scientific Discovery* (London: Hutchinson, 1959).
2. Gordon Goldsborough. "Manitoba Communities: De Salaberry (Rural Municipality)." Manitoba Historical Society, n.d. https://www.mhs.mb.ca/docs/municipalities/desalaberry.shtml.
3. Meilan Solly. "Wealth Is a Strong Predictor of Whether an Individual Pursues a Creative Profession." *Smithsonian Magazine*, April 30, 2019. https://www.smithsonianmag.com/smart-news/wealth-strong-predictor-whether-individual-pursues-creative-profession-180972072/.

Acknowledgments

Firsts are the least polished, most awkward, yet most memorable opportunities. Here come my first acknowledgments.

Thank you to Mom and Dad. You gave up your health, your dreams, and your opportunities so I can have mine. You were there for my first blunders and successes. Now let me help you with your many firsts in your lives. Thank you to my sister. You've always been there for me. You are one of the few in my life with whom I can truly share my vulnerabilities.

Thank you to my co-founder, Norman Yu. It is an honor and pleasure to be building something that matters. Your patience, honesty, and thoughtfulness throughout the start-up journey is what made things bearable.

Thank you to Mr. and Mrs. Fast from Niverville, Manitoba, who showed kindness to our family when we moved next door. I remember the first day we moved in. You knocked on our door with two frozen chickens in your hands to welcome us. You adopted us as your family and treated us as your own. Your kindness is not forgotten.

Thank you to everyone who gave me my first opportunities. Dr. Peter Younkin, you gave me my first research job and nurtured my interest in behavioral economics. Dr. Lindsay Holmgren, you looked past poor writing technique and encouraged me to protect my voice as a writer. Dr. Sujata Madan, you treated me in a human way at a time I felt judged only for achievements I didn't have. Dr. Young Jin Kim and Dr. Sojung Park, both of you took time and interest to get to know me during my exchange semester at Seoul National University and have supported me since those days. You took a genuine interest in my curiosity and enabled me to develop it into my first stepping-stones as an entrepreneur. To my mentor and friend Thomas Park, thank you for taking a chance on a naïve college student. You gave me your time and insights when I lacked common sense. You are one of the few who gives me honest, straightforward advice.

Thank you to everyone who helped me propel my career. Javier Villamizar, you hired me into your team on potential, character, and aspirations rather than my CV alone. You continue to support my career, now as an investor in my start-up. Sakshi Chhabra, you brought me on to your team and looked out for me, giving me an opportunity to start my investing career. Takumi Matsuzawa, you gave me pointers that helped me grow quickly in a short amount of time. Alexis Rog, you were patient and invested in my growth as an investor.

Thank you to my investors who took a chance on me as a first-time founder. Manan Mehta and Nitin Pachisia, you were the very first investors in my company. Not only did you support me as a founder, but as a person. I'm grateful. Thank to Aaron Grunfield and Charlie Feng, who gave me precious advice during the earliest days of my start-up. Thank you to Tala Al Jabri, Tamim Jabr, and Shruti Challa, who invested in the earliest version of the company. Thank you to Oliver Samwer, who personally took the time to encourage me to keep going as a founder during our hard times. Thanks to Jay Eum who gave me the kindest advice on quitting. Thank you to Aneel Ranadive, Jessica Xu, Charles Hung, Sanjeev Agrawal, and Leo Polovets for believing in me and being exceptionally patient with me.

You never once pressured me or harshly criticized me. Thank you to Dalton Caldwell and Aaron Epstein, who took extra time to understand the company and welcome my first start-up to Y-Combinator.

Thank you to my friends who've been here with me. Thank you to Daniel Wang. You've stuck with me through thick and thin. A true friend. You've used humor to lift me up during the down times and keep me anchored during the good. Tim White, you pushed me to explore my creative side and continued to keep me sharp. Kevin Jiang, we've jokingly said we only see each other when we travel. Our conversations and adventures are truly valued. Cedric Chane, thanks for always reminding me of gratitude, and helping me see the world in a better light. Thanks to my friends Nathan, Jinny, Gabe, and, Patrick, who love me for who I am—even the annoying parts.

Thank you to everyone involved in this book. Christina Rudloff, you picked me out of the crowd to turn my ideas into a book. Thank you to my early readers and supporters: Nir Eyal, Alok Sama, Jihoon Rim, Rian Liu, Karthik Ramanna, Sojung Park, Charlie Feng, Alexandra Donelly, Kevin Jiang, Carin-Isabel Knoop, Julie Kerr, and Mike Ross.

Finally, I thank Jesus Christ, my savior and Lord. Everything I do has meaning because of you. You've been nothing but good.

About the Author

Daniel Shin Un Kang is the author of *The Super Upside Factor*, which distills strategies used by venture capitalists to generate outsized returns—despite being wrong most of the time—but in life decisions.

He is the co-founder of a tech start-up backed by Y-Combinator. Prior to his start-up, Daniel was a venture capitalist at SoftBank Vision Fund in both Silicon Valley and London. During his tenure, he served formally as a Board Observer to Auto1 Group in Berlin. Previously, he was a consultant at Oliver Wyman and a pilot sponsored by the Department of National Defence of Canada.

Daniel received his Bachelor's of Commerce from McGill University and Master's of Public Policy from the University of Oxford. In his down time, he enjoys writing pop music, drinking coffee, and spending time with his family.

Index